A
Rendezvous
with
Destiny

Jim Janz
with

A
Rendezvous
with
Destiny

By: Jim Janz

Published by: Jim Janz with *Motivated Publishing Studios*

Copyright © 2013 Jim Janz

Jim Janz
www.MyRendezvousWithDestiny.com
jejanz@telus.net

ISBN: 978-0-9919598-0-8

Printed in the United States

Second Edition, September 2013

Edited by: Beth Parker
Proofing by: John Firth
Interior layout by: Rod Schulhauser
Cover design by: Rod Schulhauser
Project Management by: Rod Schulhauser

Dedication

To my incredible wife Sharon and our fabulous children.

Table of Contents

Acknowledgements

To My Sharon

This book is dedicated first and foremost to Sharon, my incredible life partner and wife of fifty years. Her wisdom and great ideas make our life work. She is a great wife, mother and grandmother, and has been my competent business partner for most of our married life.

On our fiftieth wedding anniversary she gave me a wall hanging with a picture of us when we were young and in the prime of our lives. On the large frame it says, "What are you doing with the rest of your life? The north, south, east and west of your life. I have only one request; that you spend it all with me!" She got an unequivocal "yes" to that request.

She talks about marriage being a lock-and-key arrangement, each spouse different, often totally opposite, but each one completing the other. She surely does that for me. She has been a huge part of all that I write about in these pages. She strengthens, comforts and encourages me when I need it most.

Mostly I want to thank her for putting up with me and all my big ideas that she has, at times, had to suffer through; for example, my deciding to write a book amidst an already very busy schedule (21 trips in the past seven months). I also owe her thanks for becoming the very competent first mate on our ocean-going vessels that keep getting bigger and bigger. She does it all so gracefully, for which I am so appreciative.

As a friend of ours says, "I am grateful but never enough."

To Our Fabulous Four Children and Their Spouses

I hope I haven't ruined your reputation too much with this book and that we'll still be friends when and if you read it. You certainly won't agree with all of it, and I don't expect you to. New generations see things differently and so they should. It will be fun to discuss the "interesting" parts by the beach next summer.

You are our pride and joy. We are so thankful for your love and caring. As we grow older, we are more appreciative every day for you and your friendship. Thank you so much for bringing nine of the most amazing grandchildren into the world! We so love every one of them. They absolutely light up our lives every time we get to see them.

In spite of the fact that we live in different parts of the world, we never seem to be disconnected. Thank God for phones, email, Facebook, texting and Skype! Even without technology, you are in our hearts every minute of every day.

Love to you all,
Dad

To Our Business Associates

I would like to acknowledge the hundreds of friends and business associates we have across North America and around the world! They are truly the most amazing group of people we could ever have been associated and affiliated with. We are continuously overwhelmed by their love and caring. It just never seems to end. You all know who you are.

We also have many friends through the philanthropic organizations that we have had the privilege of serving. You have opened so many doors for us and introduced us to other worlds. Thank you.

To our own very substantial network of business associates, and still other affiliated organizations, we say thank you. If I began to name them here, there would be no end.

Our sincere appreciation to all of you.

More will be said about these folks in later pages.

Preface

It has been difficult for me to see an increasing number of people struggling to find focus, purpose, and meaning in their lives. Finding meaning can easily be lost in the maze and the hustle and bustle of just keeping it all together these days—personally and financially.

Our major focus for the past many years has been helping people discover that meaning, whether through becoming successful in business, enhancing their personal lives, or by helping them find something to believe in that gives them the spark that inspires them to do more with their lives.

I have had the great fortune of a long and exciting career and recently I have been able to reinvent myself with the use of technology. All of this bolstered my resolve and my interest in addressing the subject of destiny.

Of late, so much has taken place, with 9/11 and the financial and social upheaval we are experiencing around the world. I presumptively felt that I may have a message that would give hope and possibly some understanding about what is happening and how we can make our way through this unique time in our history.

I hope the thoughts we share here will resonate with some of you in such a way that you become more involved in becoming part the solutions needed to resolve some of the huge challenges we face. At the same time, we must live positive, faith-filled lives as we pursue our rendezvous with destiny, or at least do more to live out the destiny we have already discovered and are fulfilling. We all can make a difference.

We welcome you to dialogue with us on our blog at www.MyRendezvousWithDestiny.com.

Destiny

Destiny is something everyone wants to discover, but is not always something that everyone knows how to find, nor do we know how to get there from here once it is found.

In these pages we will attempt to:

1. Define destiny
2. Work on discovering it, for those who do not yet have clarity on this subject
3. Find ways to "get there from here"
4. Proceed to achieve it, and then
5. Live out the destiny we have been called to fulfill

While I've been working on the subject, I discovered how big it really is. In fact, it is virtually impossible to do a full treatise on destiny in one sitting. So we'll just open the door to the power and dynamism that comes from discovering all of the elements of it, and find out what it takes to "get there from here."

I have come away from every work session uplifted, inspired and sometimes overwhelmed by the immensity of the subject. So in the few hours that we spend together, we'll definitely discover what is yet to be discovered on the subject, while we take the basics and hit a home run with them. We may fill in the blanks at another time, but sometimes it's better and even more effective to just to run with the core of the issue...

I have stripped our task down to the smallest common denominator, dealing with the most relevant principles and aspects of achieving a fulfilled life. In short, when living it to the max, this type of dynamic living spills over into the lives of others, blessing them beyond measure, and giving us a feeling of significance at the same time.

Have fun with this. Finding purpose gives peace of mind and heart.

Introduction

Is Destiny Calling You?

If you are still not sure what your calling is, this book may help you to have your rendezvous with destiny. Pressing toward the mark of your highest calling is the stuff destiny is made of, but how we find it, and how we get there from here, is our biggest challenge.

More than ever we need answers to life. At a time when so much information is coming at us every day, and when the world and its belief systems are doing 180s right before our eyes, we need to know what our calling and purpose is.

When we finally do lock into what our destiny is, our life takes on a new dimension. We become who we always wanted to become and, for some, we get to do what we have always wanted to do, but most importantly, we clearly know what our focus is, and it inspires us from the moment we wake up in the morning until we retire at night. Our legacy begins to unfold.

And yet we sometimes actually make too much of all of this.

Philosophers spin their theories, poets write songs, some people drop out of society, and some hold on tightly to the establishment. So in the end, your destiny is often just what you make it to be. Once a direction has been firmly established, it ends up being your destiny or your destination. Can it change along the way? Oh yes, as we have new revelations about what we believe, and the circumstances around us change, so does our destiny. Usually it is just a course correction but sometimes it is a total "C change."

Some people have very dogmatic feelings and beliefs about this subject that they think others must follow. For a few, this works out, but not so for most others who don't fit the mold. I personally have strong feelings and beliefs as well, but one must be flexible because we are all created so differently. One size simply does not fit all. So you'll find things in here that you love, and other things, "not so much." That is okay. You can go shopping.

> " Those who do not work on creating the future they want,
>   Often have to live with the one they are given.

Setting the Stage

Some people wonder if it is still possible to realize their destiny. Is there still time to make that childhood dream become a reality in this often chaotic and upside-down world that we live in today? Or will we soon be forced to simply survive, as in other, more primitive times?

Since the beginning of the last century, those of us in the West, and now more recently in most of the entire world, have aspired to a better life for ourselves. We in North America and Europe who've had great opportunities may be in jeopardy of losing them because we are straying from some of the principles and concepts that have been fundamental to creating an atmosphere conducive to allowing those opportunities to flourish.

It has been said that, "Life is either a daring adventure or nothing at all."

Opportunities have always and will always exist for those who stay optimistic until the end of time. They're also there for those who dare to venture out of their comfort zone to where commercial ventures and social causes are continuously calling for them to engage.

This is not a time to cower in the corner, whimpering and whining with victim mentality; rather it is a time to stand up, get engaged and fight for all that is right and good. We do this while we do what we can to hold back the flood of wrongdoing and evil that seems more prevalent than ever in our world today. As standards change and new norms and mores take hold, a new generation struggles to find meaning, and an older generation tries to stay relevant. The desire for purpose and meaning, however, still dominates our thinking.

Our objective here is to encourage those who wish to find, and then to continue to press toward, their highest calling in life.

Even though having a call to destiny may sound ominous to some, it does not mean you need to have your head down 24/7 for the rest of your life on some mission impossible. It probably does, however, call for setting aside a few extended periods of time to do what Olympic athletes have to do in order to reach their personal best and actually accomplish those goals and dreams—not just poke them with a stick.

> It is, however, important for those of us who are race horses that we do not diminish those who never want to test themselves this way. There are many other ways to find fulfilment in life.
> I know a lot of healthy, fulfilled runners who never do marathons.

We come at this from many angles, and I hope and believe that there will be an "aha" moment for you somewhere in here, when that ultimate, meaningful thing becomes totally clear, or is reconfirmed as being your destiny.

People who have heeded the call to rendezvous with their destiny have changed history throughout the ages. Being open to, and pursuing enlightenment about, the path designed for you so you can make and leave that most significant mark does not have to be drudgery, painstakingly difficult work, or even a burdensome process. Most of the time it is a joy-filled experience that brings out and utilizes your best talents, latent though they may be at this time.

Some of you may make some life-changing decisions even as we begin to define this poignant and somewhat complex subject in these opening pages.

That's how real and how close your rendezvous with destiny may be. A few slight course corrections at times is all that it takes to land you right in the center of the purpose for your life. Some people just need to be made aware that they've already found it and have been exercising their calling for years. When that discovery is made, new life is breathed into what your life course already is. New joy and fulfillment floods your being. Waking up to every new day becomes more meaningful.

Some believe their destiny was put in place before the foundations of the earth; others find it easier to believe that an ant or a queen bee has more of a destiny than they do.

> " Some believe their destiny was put in place before the foundations of the earth; others find it easier to believe that an ant or a queen bee has more of a destiny than they do.

Many of you reading this are already sure of your destiny, and like me you are always looking for ways to fine-tune it in order to do better with your calling. You may also be looking for ways to pay it forward by helping someone else find their destiny. Several people have already personally put in orders for up to 100 copies of this book for family and friends before it has seen the light of day. People have a strong desire to know their reason for passing this way, and to find ways to get there from here.

Struggling?

If you have been struggling, or if you instinctively know you could do so much more, then you are ready for a breakthrough. Making a quantum leap is a radical idea, and it requires a fundamental shift in the way you think and operate...But it is not complicated or profound.

Mozart said,

> "True genius lies in simplicity."

Chapter 1: Is Destiny Calling You?—Let's Find Out

Let's Check It out

There is more uncertainty in the world today than there has been for 70 years. Much of what we once put our faith and trust into seems to be shaken to the core. Many people have lost their financial footing, others have seen their leaders let them down or had their belief systems shaken by a post-modern era that has thrived on tearing down most of what was once fundamental to us for generations. 9/11 and recent global economic meltdowns have contributed, or have just blurred the picture for some. There isn't even the same clarity about who's on first and who's on second amongst world powers as there was in the past. You might say well, that is a good thing, and you may be right, but this kind of uncertainty is still unsettling.

How We Think Determines Everything

We should not give up on having a life of fulfillment, significance, and even financial success. Those who have a lifetime dream or purpose are for the most part less shaken by current events than those who don't, especially if that dream involves helping others or has a spiritual component to it. They know who they are and why they are here and they'll continue to pursue their mission in life in good times and bad. *In other words, they know their destiny.*

For some, big changes have to be made in order to keep their hopes and dreams alive. Others need to discover or re-discover who they are.

David Schwartz in his book *The Magic of Thinking Big* jolts people into expanding their thinking. He certainly did that for me 45 years ago, enough to cause me to share his philosophy for many years. Here is one example of how a change in thinking can revolutionize one's life.

The Dentist

A few years ago a dentist friend and business associate talked with me about his life and where it was going. It looked most likely that he was going to have a small, albeit successful, business as a one-chair dentist shop for the foreseeable future.

Often we trade the good life for the great life we've been destined to fulfill. My father in-law used to quote this simple but still profound little ditty: "Good better best never let it rest, until the good is better and the better is the best."

> Often we trade the good life for the great life we've been destined to fulfill.

After we discussed what possibilities were out there and how one's thinking could change things dramatically, there soon was another dentist working at another chair; and now there is a third in that office. Real estate investments were made with the extra cash, and when opportunities to acquire more offices became available, they led to ownership of six more dental offices throughout the Lower Mainland of Vancouver, British Columbia. I heard my dentist friend on a radio ad this week expounding on the virtues of the unique service his practice now provides to this vast group of cities nestled in a beautiful southwestern corner of Canada. Just a simple change in thinking turned him into a mega-provider of dental care to thousands of people who, until he came along, did not have that level of care available.

Today, the dentist uses a special pain-free procedure and other leading-edge concepts that attract people to his offices. His personality exudes charm throughout the organization. His practice provides jobs for about 60 people and he's lifted the profession to new heights wherever he and his dynamic wife go. She has been a big part of making this all become a reality as well. They moved from an older home on a regular lot in Vancouver to a 10-acre estate in the country. They share their beautiful place with many folks throughout the year, some of whom seldom get a chance to be out of the city except for a visit to their place. As hosts, they provide an afternoon and evening of great enjoyment, including food and entertainment.

By the way, much of this happened during the recent recession and world economic crisis, events that clouded so many people's thinking in regards to how to make their world work the way they intended. An important lesson to remember is that your dream, your vision, and your destiny do not have to be thwarted by bad economic times.

What does my friend say about his success? He says it all began with those few discussions over a coffee. A lunch or two then led to a major shift in his thinking. His goal was to offer better and unique dental care to thousands of people for whom such care would otherwise be out of reach, all in a timeframe of about six years. This is what real hope and change look like.

Because they've been able to generate extra funds, philanthropy has been a big part of their lives. This great couple helps many who are less fortunate. Many family members and friends, as well as organizations that help people in need, have been the recipients of their generosity. Would all of these people have been helped without the willingness of a "one chair dentist" to think bigger, and then follow a new dream? You decide.

What many sceptics don't understand is the ripple effect that takes place when one person dares to follow their dream and make their destiny a reality. In the end, it's not all about them as long as their heart was about serving their fellow men. I realize there are entrepreneurs who are only in it for themselves and, as a result, inflict much havoc, pain and distress on those who come within their sphere of influence. They too have found a kind of destiny. It's just not exemplary. It's also unfortunate that these people often get more than their fair share of the media ink when there are so many who provide so much to so many.

> "What many sceptics don't understand is the ripple effect that takes place when one person dares to follow their dream and make their destiny a reality.

Beirut

Several years ago, when Beirut was in turmoil, I was on a flight from Zurich to New York, sitting beside a classy gentleman from that city. I said to him, "So how do you make a living in Beirut with all the war and upheaval going on there these days?" He explained that he owned and operated a very successful spa resort on the ocean just outside of Beirut and was doing extremely well. He said most of what we were seeing in the news was happening in a relatively small area of the city.

I was taken aback and once again made to realize that life goes on regardless of man's inhumanity to man, and regardless of financial or natural disasters. The determining factor in how we come out of these situations has a lot to do with whether we have a victim mentality or an optimistic, survival perspective.

Just by the way, we had to make an emergency landing that day at the Bangor, Maine Air Force base due to a suspected fire in the hold. Stuff happens every day if you are out there stirring things up, but there is never a dull or boring moment. My 95-year-old dad used to say that the secret is to take life one day at a time with whatever it brings. He said everything always works out in the end. When someone challenged him and said, "Things are not working out for me," he replied, "Maybe not, but it isn't the end yet either."

The World Has Changed and Will Never Be the Same

People are saying the world has drastically changed and will never be the same again. They may be right, but I also believe that most of the fundamental principles that worked in the past still work for us today. They will continue to work for us in the future if they are based on the golden rule. Methods and circumstances change, but fundamental concepts and principles are timeless.

Most importantly, we must not look back. We must do what thousands of people are doing with houses today that have a good foundation; they tear down much, or in some cases all, of the superstructure, and then build something new, exciting, functional and totally updated on that foundation to meet the needs of today's world. But whenever you can, keep the foundation. It's when we destroy all the good foundations built by brilliant and wise people that we start to flounder, drift, and wonder where life is taking us.

> Most importantly, we must not look back. We must do what thousands of people are doing with houses today that have a good foundation; they tear down much, or in some cases all, of the superstructure, and then build something new, exciting, functional and totally updated on that foundation to meet the needs of today's world.

The house that was our family home during the time our kids were growing up just sold again two years ago for 2.8 million dollars. The new owners tore down the main part of the house completely, leaving the more recently constructed recreation area and indoor pool. The foundation now holds a great new, updated, solidly-built house in a desirable neighbourhood. By the way, we sold the house for less than 1/3 of that price many years ago.

For the most part, those who've found their life dream or purpose and are pursuing it are doing just fine, just as we illustrated in my dentist friend's pursuit and fulfillment of a dream. They are doing so right in the vortex of some of the most difficult economic and social upheaval we've seen in modern times.

Those who believe they are destined to make a difference are constantly looking for ways to help rectify the problems the world faces. They are always looking for dynamic opportunities to make this happen in this new and different world.

Let's Agree on the Ground Rules

Before we get into the heavy lifting here, let me say that there is never a time when you should diminish who you are, what you have done, or are now doing in life. Some of the greatest people I know are still searching for the brass ring they believe will take them to their destiny. Others have given up, and still others don't care or don't believe that they necessarily even have a destiny to fulfill. I have no issue with this kind of thinking or with wonderful friends who feel this way. They have my love, respect and appreciation because of what they mean to me personally. It's just that some of us crazies think we should do more.

Impossibilities become possibilities when destiny comes into play.

This treatise is for those who feel they have a destiny to fulfil and want to see it come to fruition. I am totally cool with someone who rejects this message because it's not for them—I can easily love them unconditionally. Someone once said, "Don't entertain any shoulds, don't let anyone should on you, don't should on anyone else, and for sure, don't should on yourself either." And don't say that too fast. Okay?

Impossibilities become possibilities when destiny comes into play.

A
Rendezvous
with
Destiny

What Do You Really Want?

Stepping up to reach for your ultimate destiny often requires that you start thinking about what you really want to accomplish in life—instead of what "common sense" says is reasonable for you to achieve.

Chapter 2: Discovery— The Fundamental Rules of Engagement

For those who are still in the hunt or have already been there and done that, let's go. For those wishing to do more to accomplish their purposes, dreams and goals, the fundamental rules of engagement have not changed and they never will.

For the past 48 years we've tried to help people do more with their lives by focussing on the possibilities available to them. It has been rewarding to see many people find their theme and their dream, and sometimes even a beam that reached into their very souls. I believe almost everyone has a destiny to fulfill if they wish to discover it and work to fulfill it. We will discuss that in depth later.

Only when you know who you are, where you are going, and only when you've found a vehicle or vehicles to take you there, do you actually have a chance of "getting there."

We've also discovered why so many people are looking for success in all the wrong places, and why so many are making the same mistakes over and over again. As a result, they keep failing in their quest for fulfilment and success in their personal lives, businesses or professions. We all know that "Insanity is doing the same things over and over again and expecting a different result." Starting over can be fun for a while, but it gets very tiring and expensive after a while and it certainly doesn't get you there from here expeditiously. But don't let that keep you from going again if you have not hit the bull's eye yet.

> Starting over can be fun for a while, but it gets very tiring and expensive after a while and it certainly doesn't get you there from here expeditiously. But don't let that keep you from going again if you have not hit the bull's eye yet.

To begin with, it's an inside job. We may be able to help with the diagnosis by reviewing many of the known but often intangible elements that are involved in the process of "getting there from here." In the end, the approach "If it is to be, it is up to me" still holds true.

When our will, our belief, and our willingness become actively engaged in the bigger picture designed by the Creator Himself, everything changes. Those with a stubborn rebellious self will have to find another way.

We all have to look inside to see:
>   how focused our purpose,
>   how intense our desire,
>   how solid our will to win,
>   how good our work ethic,
>   and how strong our faith is.

These indices, along with a strong belief that all things are possible, determine whether we are ready to achieve our God-given purpose and potential in life in a way that makes the world a better place when we pass it on to the next generation.

A question to ask is, "Have I really got my stuff together?"

Getting Ready to Fulfill Your Destiny

There is a certain something that happens when we are ready, and we are on our way to a destiny fulfilled. We are now ready to be who we need to be in order to create the energy needed to attract what is necessary to get there from here. In fact, "We've either got it or we don't!"—Whoa!

Have you ever been in a situation when someone walks into the room and the molecules literally seem to change? Or a couple strolls by and it seems like they just have it all? I love it when someone who really has it takes the mic, often in the role of a master of ceremonies or moderator, and just magically electrifies the room with their poise, their confidence, and their humour. We all know a few people who seemingly make a success of everything they touch. They have a presence that seems to literally make the ground shake a bit when they show up. Most of us are not gifted with all of that, but we can have some of it.

These movers and shakers are usually men and women of deep conviction and character, like the legendary Cliff Barrows with the Billy Graham Association, and Billy himself, of course, who is known by many of you. I had the privilege of meeting Ronald Reagan, and it was a poignant few minutes. The aura, or presence if you like, that these people have can be partly just a matter of personality. But if it's real and not just skin deep, it comes from years of doing things in a credible fashion, and from the discipline of being true to the core of a purpose-driven life.

When inner peace and balance are there, a person exudes outer poise and confidence that is visible for all to see. It also is for us all to achieve. Will we all become suave and debonair? No, but our character will shine through brilliantly and attractively, and that's all that counts.

> When inner peace and balance are there, outer poise and confidence exude and is visible for all to see. It also is for us all to achieve.

If it is all a "put on" or shallow, it crumbles the minute such persons are challenged in any way. The balloon bursts quickly. We're not talking Hollywood here.

What Do These People Have and How Did They Get It?

These people have reached a place where many of us would like to be. At times we may even envy these folks, e.g., the athlete on the podium receiving a medal, or others who are just extremely disciplined and seem to have it all together, all of the time. They are at the gym at five a.m. every morning, they eat right, they read profusely, and they have time for the important people in their lives, as well as the average person on the street.

They are the ones who reach dizzying heights of achievement. It may happen several times in their lives because even though they occasionally may crash and burn, they seldom quit; they just turn the page and do it again.

You may be one of them. If you are, congratulations! You are one of those people who has been willing to stay focused, to pay the price, to be an overcomer, to be a survivor. You found your absolutes, you know what you believe in, and you live by it! You have found your purpose, your destiny.

And if not, you are still alive, right? So let's keep going.

At the core of most of these people is a strong belief system that they passionately, albeit sometimes quietly, adhere to. It is a river that runs deep in their being that gives them the confidence to move forward regardless of the circumstances they find themselves in. It's worth spending time searching and finding that thing that helps you understand how you fit into the world and even the universe around you. You might want to start by looking up and out before you look inside. In fact, you may not find much inside worth pursuing.

And don't let anyone tell you that individual effort is a thing of the past. No, no, and no! The 11th commandment is "thou shalt not committee." Herd mentality and being politically correct eventually leads to nothingness. There are powers that would like to reduce us to a number in a database. We must try to not let that happen. In case this becomes a reality, just be salt and light wherever you may find yourself in the days to come. Globalization and the new world order are driving this agenda and it is not all it is cracked up to be. Listen and read, and you will hear the words over and over again. Find others who explain what this is really all about. Keep your head up and your purpose clear.

Going Outside Our Comfort Zone

Living outside of our comfort zone is definitely part of the deal; it's part of getting there from here. We go to every place in our lives twice, once mentally and emotionally, then physically. Imagination is one of the most powerful concepts to adopt. Like the captain of a ship, we have to know where we are going to berth next before we leave port.

To bridge the gap from here to there, we may often have to do things that are far beyond what we thought we were capable of doing, or even thought we had the ability to perform. We have to be willing to fail forward, as John Maxwell says, "If we are afraid to fail, we are also doomed to fail."

Living outside of your comfort zone is the only way to propel yourself to "that" place. It is uncomfortable and even awkward at times. Many allow pride to keep them from taking this step of visualizing. Verbalizing and actualizing the destination can be difficult when the dream is so ominous or distant that only you can see it.

Being willing to go through the tough parts where most of the derailments take place is where true achievement, purpose and destiny are birthed.

> Being willing to go through the tough parts where most of the derailments take place is where true achievement, purpose and destiny are birthed.

Some of the greatest moments in history have been the most painful for those involved. To achieve the bigger plan, we must not look for a life of ease, but rather a life of fulfillment and significance that probably involves some pain and sacrifice. At times it may seem like it will take more than you have to give.

I admire our brave military personnel around the world who don't look at the hardships they face every day, but instead are proud of their cause. They are exhilarated when one small village is released from darkness, bondage and tyranny and brought into the light of freedom; where women are able to function as human beings again, and young girls get to go to school. They gladly risk their lives for that. It's a shame when those who send them and benefit from their sacrifice forget why they sent them there.

Becoming a "Doer"

Many of you are already the doers, but like me, you frequently need a check-up from the neck up. For instance, right now I'm on a diet and fitness regime that must be well under way before this book is published in order to maintain the credibility of the thoughts and ideas expressed here. We always have something that we need help with, or need to refocus on. We all have an Achilles heel or two.

Getting up early, slipping into a pair of running shoes and shorts and hitting the workout room is not my idea of pleasure, but neither is being in ICU with tubes up my nose. A friend of mine said one day as we were puffing our way around the jogging track on a beautiful Florida morning near Disney World, "You gotta trade a feeling for a feeling." I never forgot that.

Some people have so much aversion to pain that it keeps them from giving birth to anything of substance. They never venture into training camp to get ready to go from the bleachers into the game. Over 85 percent never seriously go for it. They never even try. Only 3 percent ever even write down their goals in detail, and most never look at them after that. True long-term successes welcome the pain that comes with getting a desired result. It's often a factor in measuring their progress.

> True long-term successes welcome the pain that comes with getting a desired result. It's often a factor in measuring their progress.

We don't have to be a player on the field in every game. It's all right to be cheering from the stands for those who are doing what we are not called to, or able to do. But many of us know that we have a calling on our lives, or at least we know that we are born with seeds of greatness somewhere deep inside of us that will drive us out onto the field of battle at some point in our lives.

Getting Rid of Barriers

Let's remove some of the barriers that keep us from breaking through to our destiny.

The goal here is to remove many of the barriers that keep about 80 percent of the people in the world from accomplishing something of major significance in life.

We are reminded that the intangibles of success and achievement are timeless and sure. We are also going to take a glimpse at dozens of reasons why people succeed, or fail, in good times and bad. This will encourage the 20 percent who make it all happen to keep going and not get weary of doing well. At the same time, it will continue to encourage those who've not yet made that decision to go for it.

We must be kind and generous to those who can't go there yet, or who still just simply resist wanting to do what it takes to go there. I will say again, it's not for everybody, even though almost everyone with a dream has a chance at achievement and fulfilment. This is the case whether you are a priest, a professor, a pundit, or a producer in the market place, as long as you are willing to take on the discipline of those who do it well.

Here in the second decade of the 21st century we find ourselves in the economic and social struggle of our lives. It is one that will cast a long shadow over generations to come. How do we cope with all of this fundamental change?

We cope because, as we have already said, the intangibles of success are constant and they work in good times and bad. In addition, we may find more opportunities during these days than in any others we have encountered, provided we keep working the "glass half full" principle.

The questions we need to ask ourselves are: How long do we want it to take? How hard do we want it to be? How much unnecessary pain do we want to endure? How much do we love our stubborn, self-centred ways? How willing are we to submit ourselves to what has already been proven to work, and to those who are experienced in our area of endeavour?

NEEDED:

Ambitious, Courageous, Empathetic, Honest, Tough, Hardworking, Compassionate Leaders for Such a Time as This. Believe me, these kinds of leaders are scarce. If your call to destiny includes some of the above, I encourage you to enlist.

The world needs the people reading this right now. The exciting thing is that, contrary to public opinion, and because of what we have just discussed, there's an extreme dearth of passionate, character-driven leadership today that desperately needs to be filled. So please give some thought to moving upward and onward. Some of you need to do it again, regardless of the hurts and regardless of the failures of the past.

Take another shot at it. If you have any inkling that you might be able to be of value on a winning team or as a team leader in the game of life, you are so needed. Those of you who are entrepreneurial, suck it up and go for it. You are the engine of the economy; don't let anyone disparage you for fulfilling that mandate. Hopefully, it won't take major brain surgery to get you ready to play again because there are so many things these days to hold us back and sidetrack us, not the least of which is the doom and gloom we hear and read about in the media day in and day out. Well-meaning friends can be the biggest stumbling block.

> Those of you who are entrepreneurial, suck it up and go for it. You are the engine of the economy; don't let anyone disparage you for fulfilling that mandate.

A familiar statement that fits our conversation here is that there are three groups of people in the world: the group that makes things happen, the group that watches things happen, and the group that wonders what happened. We all find ourselves in one of those groups, and in some cases all of those groups, depending on the situation.

As we said earlier, we also know a very small group of people who march to a different drummer and who make a difference every day. We'll explore what they have and what they do in the chapters ahead.

They have a few main things going for them, but there are also myriads of other things that are vital to the process of getting there and staying there, and finishing well. Some of these rather simple factors will cause an "aha" moment for us but also may be the very thing that might have kept us in the stands if we didn't get it.

Lifelong serious halitosis can screw it all up for you if not dealt with. Try a little honey and cinnamon. I'm serious. Don't be afraid of problems, as there are solutions for most of them, and when you cease to have problems, you are dead.

"Problems are the normal state of life." Charley Jones

It's Going to Take a Ferocious Run – Stay with Me!

Some of you know your destiny but would just like to shorten the journey. Some of my friends I talk about in this book just may have the answer.

The focus in these pages is to help people achieve meaningful, realistic, and at times lofty objectives. To do that, we'll take another look at the many timeless and sometimes intangible principles that have been effective for those who've achieved great and mighty things. But while we still use timeless principles, we must also learn how to maximize the use of modern technology as well as social media to reach those unfulfilled dreams and goals.

Last but not least, it takes a ferocious run at it to achieve it all. If you see three new clients a week, you may have to see three a day for a few months. Try ninety days. When I started in business I broke many records, not because I was more talented or skilful or more mature. It was simply because I filled five to six time slots a day, five to seven days a week, with goal-oriented activities. Others thought they were working hard doing two to three a week.

How many presentations should you do? As many as you possibly can. You have to do whatever it takes to reach that coveted goal or destination. I speak from experience.

I usually got up at 5 a.m. to get myself ready for the day, physically and spiritually (I'm lazing around today: I didn't get up till 5:30). I did prep and called to confirm appointments so I didn't waste time on no-shows and missed cues. Then to a 7:00 or 7:30 breakfast appointment; then 9:30, 11:00, 12:30 and 2:30. I hustled home to pick up the kids from school, help with transportation and attend the kids' sporting events, etc. It was family time from 3:30 to 7:00, and then out for appointments and meetings till late. Friday night was family night and one weekend a month a vacation at home or away—skiing, the lake house or whatever was on the agenda.

I travel a great deal. I woke up one morning after speaking in nine cities in nine days and didn't know where I was. I had to look in the phone book to find out. I called home one evening and was scolded by my teenaged daughter for being late for dinner. I was in Amsterdam. They were used to me being away. I kept it short. I was away only three days on that trip. I took the Concorde from Washington DC, three hours and 22 minutes to London, England. Ironically my daughter has lived overseas for years now and is arriving home this morning from Singapore in two hours.

We seldom feel satisfied about our efforts until we've left it all on the field. An all-star professional football player friend of mine was playing in another city. I watched him on television as he gave it his all on that very hot day. He was hit hard after a brutal tackle and didn't get up. The trainers came out and he lay there for some time.

I was out running with him the next morning and I asked, "What was your injury last night?"

He said that he wasn't injured. Then I asked, "So what was the long stint on the field with the medics?"

"Oh that!" he said, "I had just given it all I had and had no gas left in the tank. I needed a rest because I knew I couldn't execute the next plays if I didn't take a breather." My friend single-handedly won that game for the team on that next series of plays. He didn't just play by the book; he did whatever it took. I loved Don for that. He taught me to play like that in my business.

People who try to get away with as little effort as possible end up with very little.

> People who try to get away with as little effort as possible end up with very little.

The Times We Live in

We can't go down this road to extraordinary achievement without seriously addressing the uncertain times we live in, and how to survive them. One can no longer enter into a dialogue on these subjects and expect to take several years to publish because of how quickly things change. When I started working on this book some years ago, life was good. Some storm clouds were on the horizon, but no one seemed to anticipate our world economy going into a tailspin of gigantic proportions, or millions of people taking to the streets in an attempt to change regimes and overthrow dictators with Facebook and Twitter. Such devices hadn't even been invented yet.

Don't Kill the Goose

I have friends who've been able to give away hundreds of millions of dollars for hospitals and research, and for schools and orphanages in impoverished areas around the world. We must never minimize the possibility for ambitious good people to do these things. Bill and Melinda Gates and Warren and Mary Buffett are good examples, as well as people like Rich and Helen DeVos, Jay and Betty Van Andel, Jimmy Pattison, John Maxwell, and Jim and Nancy Dornan. These are just a few of the thousands of the often unheralded entrepreneurs who have and are changing the world with their generosity. In fact, the giving principle is the number-one principle to adopt if you really want to get there from here without using devious and nefarious means to get there.

> The giving principle is the number-one principle to adopt if you really want to get there from here without using devious and nefarious means to get there.

I recognize that the free market system has at times failed because it hasn't been responsible with what it was entrusted with. But let's not throw the baby out with the bath water just because of the few who let the two deadly sins of ego and greed take them down, along with so many other innocent people. Let's make sure we don't kill the system while we work on curing its ills.

Pitfalls and Shortcuts

If you have the desire and the will to be a serious philanthropist, go for it! Pitfalls and shortcuts will not get you there faster.

Shortcuts can lengthen the journey immensely. Many of you know the Old Testament story of the children of Israel going to what they believed was their Promised Land. Because of their lack of willingness to keep their actions, attitudes, and faith intact and on track, it took them 40 years to do an 11-day trip. Rebellion might be fun for a while, but in the end, it will shut you out of what is best for your life. They had to leave the task to the next generation, who learned from their mistakes. The original group never saw their Promised Land.

What is keeping you from seeing your "promised land"?

If you are angry or blaming someone else for your lack of success, then you are in the desert. That's what these folks were doing. Watch out, once more, for victim mentality.

> "If you are angry or blaming someone else for your lack of success, then you are in the desert. That's what these folks were doing. Watch out, once more, for victim mentality.

If you want to see your promised land and you already know where it is, then do what is right, don't be rebellious, and keep the faith. And would you please commit to just getting off first base? Many people don't know that there are certain actions and beliefs that virtually guarantee success; the first and perhaps the biggest is believing it can happen to them. The second is getting started. The rest we'll cover here in depth.

So come and take this journey with me. Together we'll be reminded of some fundamental timeless principles. At the same time, we'll learn about new and exciting ways to find or refurbish our destiny, and then find a way to "get there from here." Read on.

A
Rendezvous
with
Destiny

Barriers?

Consider this elegant solution:

"Most barriers are imaginary."

Chapter 3: Survival—Learning to Survive Is a Big Part of One's Destiny

Even though we all know all things are possible, there are times on our journey towards our destiny when it will be just about survival.

Sometimes It's All about Survival

During these worrisome days of economic, political, and moral upheaval, many of us occasionally find ourselves in a survival mode. So if you find yourself there any time soon, here are some tips that might help.

"Slumpy" thinking can be even more harmful to you when the chips are down than the actual circumstances you find yourself in. It's hard not to think that way when business is generally down, or when your industry or your line of work is specifically hit by a downturn. This also applies to personal, financial, and health-related issues.

During the gas shortage in 1975, car sales went into the dumper—particularly gas-guzzling cars. A dealer in the Anaheim area was thriving during this time. A friend of mine asked him what he was doing, in as much as he was selling lots of vehicles of all shapes and sizes. He said, "I don't believe in 'slumpy' thinking. We just don't participate in that kind of thinking, and the results are consistently amazing!

"As dealerships in the area closed I hired their top sales and service people. I advertised that there was no recession at XYZ dealership, and as other dealers dropped their best advertising spots, I took them. I installed new and brighter lights on the sales lot along with upbeat music. Business was booming and continued to do so for years to come."

Our thought process has so much to do with how we live our lives and how things work out for us. So often I hear people say when something goes bump in the night, "I knew that would happen, I just knew it." Well, guess what, it did, and it will continue to until they look at things from a different perspective. Some people dig a big hole before they are willing to admit that they may at times have something to do with their misfortunes.

Trite but true: "If you find yourself in a deep hole, stop digging."

If you find yourself in a deep hole, stop digging.

Upbeat Your Activities

The tendency is to slow down and even stop our activities when we hit the wall and all seems to be dark in our businesses or personal lives. It is during these times that we need to be reminded that, "There is always a way."

During the same 1975 fuel shortages, an acquaintance of mine who owned a service station was about ready to close shop. He came to me and asked if I could see anything that he could do to save his business. Another friend and I went over and took a look. We found five slightly rusted, long metal poles lying in the back of the station and several arc lights inside in a back room full of junk. We brought another friend over who was in the concrete business to help us dig some holes and then anchor the five newly sanded and painted poles into concrete bases.

We purchased a Canadian flag, a provincial flag, two corporate flags and a U.S. flag. We cleaned up the lights, anchored them and trained them on the poles and the flags. With new paint on the building, brilliantly cleaned-up windows and some newly hired young people with white shirts, beige slacks and running shoes, the place was ready to go. A source of fuel was "found" and there was a grand re-opening.

The place went nuts and it never stopped. Several years later the business sold for seven figures! The total cost for the upgrade? About $650.00 plus a bunch of free labour.

Remove and Replace

Remove all lowering, limiting, defeating thoughts from your mind and replace them with uplifting, unlimited, winning thoughts.

> Remove all lowering, limiting, defeating thoughts from your mind and replace them with uplifting, unlimited, winning thoughts.

A slump is more mental than real, even when there are often many tangible indices that would support having a slump. It is so easy to slip into lowering, limiting, defeating thoughts when the clouds are hanging low and it gets really dark.

This is when you work at uplifting, unlimited winning thoughts. I have seen so many sports teams go through a slump, and then saw what happens when leadership takes on a new thinking process. It blows the overcast sky away, the team lurches back to life and an unparalleled winning streak ensues.

> I have seen so many sports teams go through a slump, and then saw what happens when leadership takes on a new thinking process. It blows the overcast sky away, the team lurches back to life and an unparalleled winning streak ensues.

I have seen a change in quarterbacks at half time, or anytime for that matter, and instantly, amazing things begin to happen! I watched a team come back from a 32-to-0 halftime score to a 34-to-32 win, just with a change of quarterbacks at half time. More about this later. All it takes sometimes is one inspirational person at the helm. With everything else staying the same, you have a colossal change in activity and productivity.

That can happen to you. You may have to be your own leader or get yourself to listen to a CD, read a book, or attend a function. Sometimes within an hour the sky begins to clear and sun shines once more.

Discouragement won't help either. You might say, "Well, you can't help getting discouraged when the bottom drops out." That may be true, but it is an attitude that can be managed. The key is to find a way to work yourself out of it. Find help: listen, read, consult with friends or professionals, or even get some prescription meds if you need them for a while. I do have great empathy for those who get ravaged by discouragement or depression due to real traumas in their lives. It's tough to crawl out of it sometimes, but everything that can be done should be done.

Flying over the Rocky Mountains several years ago, we ran into serious turbulence. The plane lurched and slammed completely onto its side, shuddered and finally straightened out, only to do it once more on the other side a few seconds later. It was scary even for a veteran flyer like me, but we made it, obviously. I'm glad, however, that in the middle of all that slamming and banging around, the pilots didn't come through the door of the cockpit and say, "We quit; we're discouraged! Nobody ever told us it would get this bad."

You might say that's ridiculous. Well, maybe, except trauma is trauma and when it happens to us we have to be strong and do our best to avoid discouragement. As a leader, and we all are a leader to someone, discouragement is a luxury we can't afford too often if our destiny is to be realized.

Visualize, Verbalize and Actualize

See it, say it, and seize it. These are the fundamentals of all achievement.

See it, say it, and seize it. These are the fundamentals of all achievement.

I had a friend in Winnipeg, Manitoba, who had a picture of a GMC motorhome on his fridge when I visited him many years ago. His station in life at that time did not reflect that kind of a luxury any time soon, but the picture remained from one visit to the next and even into the next year.

I asked him, "What's the deal with the motor home?"

He said, "It's my dream and I'm going to have one soon."

An ad jumped off the page for a used one, and my friend went down the road to check it out. It was beautiful and the price was within range. But even though his wife agreed that it was a total go, he hesitated, and the motorhome was sold the next day.

Weeks, maybe even months later, they were on their way to Minneapolis to visit friends and business associates. Out of the corner of their eyes they spotted a GMC motorhome off to the side in a rather small car lot. It was another beauty, about the same price as the other one, but this time my friend said, "We'll take it. There is something about this vehicle that just sings with me."

He said to the dealer, "This unit looks just like the one I have on my fridge."

The dealer said, "I've got news for you. It is the one on your fridge." This was the unit they used to do the initial promotional brochures! There, on the side of the highway in an obscure location…you figure it out. They had visualized it, verbalized it, and then actualized it by watching for the right vehicle to show up. In the meantime, my friend kept working at his business so they could afford it. This may seem like hocus-pocus, but don't knock it till you've tried it. I could fill a book with stories like this. Just think about the bigger things that have happened to you. What preceded them? Were they first a dream? Did you visualize the results?

The same couple was looking at show homes and fell in love with one. The brochure went up on the fridge because, once again, it was a little premature to be going there right then. The house sold. About two years later, they saw an ad in the paper for a house just like the one they had loved so much. Down the road they went and, you guessed it, it was the same house being re-sold. They lived there for many years.

Most of the greats had a vision, or they purposefully envisioned great things. In good times and bad, their visions became a reality. Churchill was not going to go down to defeat to the powerful modern Nazi forces, and he said so from his bunker in central London, which many of you have probably visited. He said, "We will win in the air, we will win on the sea, and we will win on dry land"—as the bombs were furiously pummelling the city and the country.

That belief and those faith-filled words kept the British forces in a winning posture and, as help came from Canada and the U.S. to help defeat the Nazis, Britain lived to see its finest days. Be sure you are visualising, verbalizing, and actualizing what you want, even in your darkest hours, because you'll probably get it.

When I first was introduced to the power of the subconscious mind, I felt it might be in conflict with my religious beliefs until

I realized that it too was designed by my Creator, just like all of the other miraculously and meticulously designed aspects of my body, soul and spirit.

When times are tough and survival is the only thing on your agenda, it's difficult to think your way out of the circumstances of the day to another place where things are better. But those who do, survive; they survive well and expeditiously—your choice, once again.

When times are tough and survival is the only thing on your agenda, it's difficult to think your way out of the circumstances of the day to another place where things are better, but those who do, survive.

Inspire Those around You

When everything is down, somebody has to get up for the game. It happens in the boardrooms, the bedrooms, the locker rooms, in the coffee shops and on the streets of our cities every day. Someone says, "Enough is enough, we're moving out of this mess and I'm going to lead the way."

Denver: half time, many years ago. The Denver Broncos were down 32-0 to the fledgling Seattle Seahawks. The new quarterback comes in. Craig Morton is on the side lines, with the whole team in a huddle. You can hear him screaming at the team that they were not going down to defeat to this young Seattle Seahawk team. He shouted to his cohorts, "We are going to win this game! We are going to win this game!"

Some fans had already gone home. They were humiliated and disgusted. Suddenly a team who couldn't catch a pass, who couldn't run more than two yards at a time in the first half, was catching every pass and running 10 to 15 yards per play. They won the game 34-32. One inspirational individual dared to see, and to speak about winning, when everything around them screamed that it was a losing proposition.

What changed? One person with belief in the middle of an untenable situation said, "We are not going to be defeated, we have what it takes to win and we are going to do it now."

Do you have what it takes to win? If not, we will help.

It is the Olympics, sometime in the 60s. The Japanese gymnastic team is headed for a gold medal. In the second last heat, their star performer lands awkwardly and breaks his ankle. Off to hospital he goes, leaving his dejected team behind him as their hopes for the gold evaporate before their eyes.

They gather later in the hospital. The patient tells them that they are going to win and he's going to perform. As they viewed him there with his leg in a sling, it all seemed rather far-fetched. In the wee hours of the morning, the athlete quietly made his way out of the hospital on crutches, grabbed a cab to the Olympic Stadium and was there when his team arrived the next morning. In serious pain and with perspiration pouring down his brow, he announced he would attempt to perform.

His time finally came, and to an absolutely hushed crowd the young man made his way slowly to the performing area on crutches.

He dropped the crutches and grabbed the performing bars and began his routine, up and around and over the bar with a perfection that only the best in the world can perform. The crowd was on its feet, the noise deafening, and then suddenly all went totally quiet as he came to the dismount that broken his ankle the day before.

It was executed perfectly, and then he immediately fainted in a heap on the landing pad. The next thing we saw, he was waving off the crowd around him so he could see the leader board. He propped himself up on one elbow and writhed in excruciating pain. He needed a 9.2 average to win.

Finally the scores began to show up: 8.9—the crowd gasped—9.1 9.4 9.3 9.3 9.2.

There are times when, in order to survive, we have to leave it all on the field.

There are times when, in order to survive, we have to leave it all on the field.

Value Yourself Highly

Most of us have a tendency to be down on ourselves and think we are the fault of all that is wrong with our world. That is when I look at my heroes and I take heart.

Churchill would have never made it through military school if his father had not been Sir Randolph Churchill. He was a rascal. Most of what we know about Churchill happened after he was 65. About exercise he once said, "I don't run if I can walk, and I don't walk if I can stand, and I don't stand if I can sit down." Ambitious lad.

David, the Old Testament King, got carried away with the lady next door. He sent her husband to the front lines to be killed so he could continue his tryst. He was said to be a man after God's own heart after he sincerely repented of all of that.

Moses' first act after becoming the leader of his people was murder. How do you figure? Just in case you don't know, he wrote most of the Old Testament and was responsible for communicating the 10 commandments to the world!

The Apostle Paul was killing Christians on weekends for a part-time job before he was blinded by a bright light on the way to Damascus.

Most of the greats I have ever known or read about had some serious blemishes and glitches in their lives. They still made it through the rain and so can you.

We just have to pull ourselves up by our bootstraps to our full height every day and know that we are just as good as the next guy and get on with it. When we are committed to doing things right, even though it is a constant struggle, we soon feel levels of confidence and self-esteem that allow us to start getting it done in style.

> " We just have to pull ourselves up by our bootstraps to our full height every day and know that we are just as good as the next guy and get on with it.

Excel and Be Different

To survive we sometimes have to leave the crowd of complaining, snivelling and whining souls behind. Some actually like wallowing in their misery.

It's hard to step out and be thought of as different or a dreamer. I've never met a true success who was more interested in hanging with the crowd than in getting it done in spite of the odds. Be willing to excel if it's in you to do it.

> " Be willing to excel if it's in you to do it.

Be Enthusiastic. It makes you stand out in the crowd. Churchill once stopped to talk with two guys working on a construction site. He said, "What are you doing?" One said, "I'm digging a damn ditch." Another said, "I'm building a cathedral, sir!"

Churchill also said, "At the base and birth of every successful venture you will find an enthusiast."

Be Committed. Stay until the job is done, not until the clock hits a certain hour. People who are truly committed are rare. You find them in amongst the 5% range and always in the winner's circle.

Be Involved. The game isn't played from the sidelines; it's played on the field. Fear and lack of self-esteem keeps us from getting involved. Armchair quarterbacks don't make the award ceremonies.

It was a hot day in northern California and we were on a family vacation. The pool at the hotel was our first stop late in the afternoon. Three girls showed up at the pool to "go swimming." One went in up to her ankles and then went back to the lounge chair. A second got in up to her midriff and gasped that water was too cold. She too hit the lounge chair. A third walked briskly to the diving board and dove in. She was full of exclamation marks about how great it was to cool off this way and soon had a volleyball game going in one end of the pool. The one girl on the lounge chair said to the other, "Sure looks like fun!"

People who are committed have more fun and feel more engaged and complete than those who stay around the edges and wish they were part of the action.

Be a Starter. Don't be afraid to be the first one in. Someone has to lead.

Learn everything you can about the enterprise you find yourself in. You can't excel or survive if you are ignorant about the job you are trying to do. All you have to do is run a little faster, know a little bit more, and network a little more effectively to be ahead of the competition. You'll increase your chances of survival by 100 %.

After you have analyzed the situation realistically and devised a plan of action, you are on your way to a better day. Survival is about attitude, creativity, guts, and putting your boots into action. Accept the losses, and the pain, and dare to move on to bigger, better and more prosperous and health-filled days. Give survival a chance.

> Survival is about attitude, creativity, guts, and putting your boots into action. Accept the losses, and the pain, and dare to move on to bigger, better and more prosperous and health-filled days. Give survival a chance.

Chapter 4: Fear Must Be Conquered

Fear must be conquered before destiny can be fulfilled.

Many people live lives filled with fear and trepidation. They're worried about what other people think, afraid they are being politically incorrect, fearful of making a mistake or making a wrong turn, constantly comparing themselves with those who seem to be so much better than they.

Truth be known, many are really just trapped in the box of popular social norms. They live with constant fear that their words or actions might trigger a lack of acceptance that might cause them to fall out of favour. We all have fears and we need to take them down.

Some are fearful of whom they are seen with, fearful of moving too fast, or too slow, intimidated by the driver behind them who wants to pass, afraid of making a U-turn when it's the only practical thing to do. "Go back, for pity's sake; you're lost."

Some are fearful of having too little, or of having too much; others are fearful of driving the wrong car, or living in the wrong house or neighbourhood; or, God forbid, of wearing the wrong thing. I've seen this cause panic and trauma beyond imagination. We often fear things like public speaking, failure and even success. We become concerned about living up to our successes.

Both fear and insecurity need to be conquered because fear is the paralyzer of action and progress. We wouldn't want it said of us that we had great talent and ability, and could have accomplished great things, but our fearful heart kept us from fulfilling our destiny.

> Both fear and insecurity need to be conquered because fear is the paralyzer of action and progress.

Every year in the fall we have a tradition of taking whatever grandchildren are around to the Pacific National Exhibition. Our two older grandsons haven't missed since they were little boys, and they're now in their twenties and bring their girlfriends with them.

This past fall, our other daughter's three kids came and one of them is quite fearful of going on the rides. He asked if there were darts or shuffleboard instead. The other kids said, "Oh no, we are going on the scariest rides here." For almost two hours they terrorized this poor kid as they swirled and plunged on death-defying rides. When we got back to the car, he said, "That's the most fun I have had in ages. I don't know why I was so afraid."

The interesting thing is that this young man is not afraid to speak in front of thousands; he plays soccer at the highest levels, and rock climbs. He does things that I'm sure many of us would cringe at the thought of doing. He's just a bit more rounded now, according to his cousins. I'm sure he could be of help to them in other areas. I love those grandkids and am so proud of every one of them!

Knowing the truth and applying it by faith conquers all fear. Knowing the truth about who you are, what or who you believe in, and where you will end up when you eventually pass from the scene, dissolves much of the angst that we live with daily.

Knowing the truth gives you the poise and confidence you need to go boldly into the marketplace to face the giants and the mountains waiting there for you to conquer in every endeavour, en route to where you want to go or what you want to accomplish.

Knowing the truth gives you the poise and confidence you need to go boldly into the marketplace to face the giants and the mountains waiting there for you to conquer in every endeavour, en route to where you want to go or what you want to accomplish.

No worthwhile endeavour comes without its enormous challenges, challenges that only the fearless can overcome. Truth bolsters courage and confidence, and dispels fear. Courage, however, is not the absence of fear, but action in spite of fear. We all have fears to dispel.

I would not be here if my grandfather had not fearlessly risked his life by travelling on foot from up near the Ukraine to Moscow for weeks to connect with a contact he had there. The contact then helped him with visas and passports so he and his family could escape from Russia. He slept in culverts during the day and walked at night. It took over a month to make the trip. They came out on the trains you saw in the motion picture *Dr. Zhivago*. My grandfather knew no fear. He was a man of great faith and bold action.

Courage, however, is not the absence of fear, but action in spite of fear.

Do the thing you fear the most, and the death of fear is certain. Just do it now. Fear itself can bring on calamities of grave proportions. Even Job said, "The very thing I feared the most came upon me." Be careful what you fear! Insecurity is a form of fear, and is in constant need of reassurance and affirmation. Many times the smallest comment or oversight seems offensive and creates a reaction. Insecurity is deadly; to overcome it we must get our eyes off ourselves and onto others.

> Do the thing you fear the most, and the death of fear is certain.

Be bold, but don't be brash. Boldness is a good trait as long as it does not overpower or diminish others in the process. One can be bold and fearless and still be loving and kind. Some of the boldest people I know are the kindest, most giving, most people-centred I know.

Fear evaporates when you have a BHAG (Big Hairy Audacious Goal). A BHAG sets you on fire and your passion for it overrides your fears. We do things we never thought we could do when we have a BHAG: we get up earlier, we call people on our chicken list, and we even walk faster.

Chapter 5: Is Financial Freedom Part of Your Destiny?

Without the financial piece in place, nothing works. Without financial peace we are in constant turmoil.

It's difficult to think of finding and fulfilling one's destiny without having the financial piece of our lives in order. Finances dominate our lives, whether we like it or not. In the extreme, we either suffer from stress because of the constant lack of money, or we are in hot pursuit of it for whatever reason. In the first extreme, we often find those who are bitter, jealous, envious, self-righteous or pious. In the other extreme, we often find that pride, arrogance, materialism, ego and greed are dominant.

The Parable of the Talents sums it up. It has nothing to do with how much we have, but whether or not we are good stewards of what we have been given. God seems to get a little upset with those who don't manage it well.

> God seems to get a little upset with those who don't manage it well.

Somewhere in the middle there is an amazing group of people, people who are understanding, generous, caring, and fulfilled, and who are ever so thankful for the blessings they have received. Many of them have just made an average wage, some have become professionals or entrepreneurs and done well financially, but ultimately, all of them managed what they made carefully and skilfully. Most are extremely generous. Spending was very low on their list of priorities, saving was high, and giving was highest. In other words, make as much as you can, save as much as you can, and give as much as you can. Notice the order. This clarifies the issue clearly and simply.

We seldom talk out loud about our financial well-being in real terms, and yet we must all deal with it if our destiny is to be fulfilled. Mother Teresa and her organization raised millions of dollars to support her work on the streets of Calcutta. Where did it come from? How was it raised? How does that fit our image of her and her work? Nothing in our world happens without garnering and managing funds to support it or make it happen, period. So let's quit being so hypocritical and shy about finding the best way for each of us to become financially sound. Remember, it does not happen by accident or by osmosis. You might hear that a few more times here along the way

> We seldom talk out loud about our financial well-being in real terms, and yet we must all deal with it if our destiny is to be fulfilled.

Financially speaking, many people today live lives of quiet desperation. Life has taken some unfortunate turns for many thousands of folks recently, as we've already mentioned. For others, there's a lot of concern and trepidation hanging in the air about the future. Many have suffered substantially, and almost all of us have been affected by the worldwide financial crisis. Those who managed best, suffered least.

I saw a 19-year-old on TV recently who saved his first dime at four years of age and saved 10 to 20 percent of everything he made from allowances and wages since that day. He bought his first fixer-upper house at 14; he now has four of them, three almost paid for. He lives frugally and is financially free at 19. He still lives at home but, get this, he actually pays room and board! What a novel idea. He's also enrolled in a MBA program.

The objective of this section is to help those who may not yet have taken the time to create a clearly defined, step-by-step approach to reaching a place of financial peace and freedom in their lives. They have just ignored or squelched it in hopes it would pan out somehow! Nada.

Money and finances are a huge part of our lives and we cannot put our head in the sand and hope it just works out for us. We have to deal with it. With destiny comes discipline and with discipline comes positive results.

If you don't have financial peace of mind as one of your objectives, you'll never have it. You and your family will suffer for it, as will others you could have helped if you had put your personal financial act together. It's never too late. Col. Sanders got started at 65. I've seen others do it at 70 and live well into their eighties.

There is so much hypocrisy and misinformation being touted every day regarding money. It confuses people no end. Just recently when I was in Seattle, Washington, an extremely well-known politician stayed in the hotel next to mine. He constantly berates the rich and the top 1 percent, yet he held two fundraisers there with dozens of millionaires and billionaires paying $38,000 a plate to have dinner with him. Could not that money have been spent helping the people he espouses to champion? I wonder how many poor people in Seattle could have been fed, and for how long, with the millions he took out of there in one day. And he's held over 300 of these! Every party and politician does it. No fingers pointed.

Unfortunately, the lines are blurrier today than they've ever been, but the principles are the same. I believe and hope that some sanity returns once again to the economic community. Armageddon may be close, but it's not here yet. Work like it is never coming and live like it may come today.

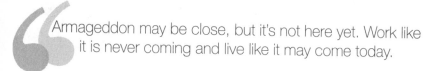

Armageddon may be close, but it's not here yet. Work like it is never coming and live like it may come today.

Maturity Is Learning to Live with Uncertainty

If you really have a desire to be financially free, you can have a good foundation in place in 36 to 48 months. I've known people who have tripled and quadrupled their net worth and their cash flow in that period of time, and you can too. Everything begins with a decision, a commitment, and a plan of action, as we've reiterated so often in these pages. We are all part of the problem or part of the solution when it comes to money.

One of the biggest hurdles to overcome is thinking that achieving financial bliss is so elusive that it can't be done anymore, or that it can only happen for the privileged few. Nada. I hear some young people say that the previous generation raped the world of its wealth and there's no opportunity left for them. They say that while down the street a new immigrant who can hardly speak the language is flourishing in his new business venture, providing goods and services, and offering employment to dozens of folks in the neighbourhood.

I hired a car and a driver in Paris a few weeks ago. The driver owned a fleet of seven vehicles, amongst them, a Mercedes and some limos. He saved his money from childhood with the dream of owning a business one day and just two years ago he bought the company. He is 28. He used his creative genius by making friends with young people in the travel business who work for cruise lines as hotel concierges and in tour offices and similar places. They all refer their customers to him. He is busy 24/7, recession or not.

> One of the biggest hurdles to overcome is thinking that achieving financial bliss is so elusive that it can't be done anymore, or that it can only happen for the privileged few.

So who recommended him to us? His friend, the young concierge at the Charles de Gaulle Airport Marriott. And 250 euros later we had great transportation around Paris, he made a good income for those few hours, and we booked him for another gig with friends a week later while passing through Paris again.

Once you have the fundamentals in place and you're on the right track, it's just a timing issue. It's a shift in thinking. For some, it's huge shift in thinking. It may take a willingness to sacrifice, to go without for a while. I often say, "You either go now and pay, and pay, and pay later, or you pay the price now and go later hassle free."

Some people literally let their daily Starbucks coffee, six-packs of beer, bottles of wine, or the sale sign in the window (with the resulting credit card debt) get in the way of their future financial well-being. In some cases, just saving that amount of money is the difference between financial freedom or financial stress and regret down the road.

For those of you who've already successfully gone down this road, I recommend you take the time to do this easy read in order to help the people you know, including your kids and grandkids, gain a better understanding of how they can become financially free. You are only a victim if you declare yourself as one. Victim mentality keeps you stuck where you are forever. Let's move out of Dodge!

The media has capitalized on almost everyone's desire to reach the jackpot with smash hit TV shows like *Who Wants to Be a Millionaire* that rated highly, week after week and month after month. Fifty thousand people are purported to have signed up for the first *Survivor* show, where the winner walked away with a million plus. Many multi-million-dollar lotteries are sold out long before their due date. Most people, if they were honest, would like to play even if they don't.

We see 22-year-olds making $5,000,000 and more per year chasing a little piece of rubber around the ice or chucking that orange ball into a hoop, while most of us find ourselves without the genetic disposition or the psychological bent to even attempt that kind of thing. So what can we ordinary folks do?

The "dot com" millionaires were all over the front pages for a while, making us think that everyone was getting rich quick, except us. Now finding an online income is the latest rage, and of course, if you worked for Facebook, your fortunes recently increased dramatically—at least for a few days!

Some ask or suggest, "Should we even be going down this road?"

Without getting too philosophical too early in our discourse, it may beg the question, "Is this desire to create wealth or financial freedom even a good thing?"

In itself, pursuing wealth is benign and generally a good thing; however, when it enters the "get rich quick" syndrome, or the idea that one can get "something for nothing," we move into the troubled waters demonstrated all too well by the dot com crash.

> In itself, pursuing wealth is benign and generally a good thing; however, when it enters the "get rich quick" syndrome, or the idea that one can get "something for nothing," we move into the troubled waters demonstrated all too well by the dot com crash.

It can also become so much of an obsession that it drives all other aspects of our lives into the shadows. More divorces have occurred because some cowboy made the pursuit of money his everything. The "Manufacturers Handbook" (The Bible) says, "What shall it profit a man(/woman) if he gains the whole world but loses his own soul?" I recently saw a documentary about a gentleman who won a 300-million-dollar lottery. He said he would do anything to go back to the life he had before. He lost his wife, his most precious granddaughter, and everything that was important to him as a direct result of winning the money.

It's important to have balance and perspective, lest we lose our way en route to the "prize"—many have. Many a destiny has been sidelined by these issues.

Selfish ambition and greed never lead to long-term financial freedom. I have acquaintances in jail today because of their involvement in Ponzi schemes and other forms of illegal promotional programs that profited them disproportionately while causing the investor to lose all or most of their money.

The late Zig Ziglar said, "If you help enough people get what they want, you will always have what you want." That is true wealth but very difficult to get one's head around. We are so designed to survive and to go after what we want that we can't imagine helping others first. Have you ever gone Christmas shopping and come home only with things for yourself? I have.

Having Said All That...

Having said all that, many of us neglect doing the things that we need to do in order to achieve the level of financial stability and the financial well-being that we are capable of. It is financial freedom that is, or will be, an essential part of our lives moving forward.

When the kids start to want vehicles and are looking at schools with a $50,000 price tag for tuition that we would like them to be able to attend, how does that work if we haven't been open to the idea of accumulating a few extra dollars along the way? These

49

seem like impossible mountains to climb, but they're not. All things are possible if you believe! One more time, "With man it is impossible but with God all things are possible."

> All things are possible if you believe! One more time, "With man it is impossible but with God all things are possible."

We can be well on our way to a good place financially in just a few short months, provided we change our thinking and our focus to what is possible, instead of what seems impossible. By just doing some simple things we can begin to turn our entire financial future around, while at the same time getting some immediate financial relief.

Let's look at some real and doable concepts that can help you get there from here financially. These are ideas and concepts that can launch you into an orbit that could actually categorize you as being "financially free," at least by the following definition.

> Financial freedom has been defined by "how long you can live at your desired lifestyle without anyone in your household having to formally work for a living."
> R. Kyosaki

This does not mean they do not work. Most work very hard because they still have unreached goals, huge causes they want to support, and many responsibilities they have, such as families who depend on jobs they may be providing.

Most people work for money instead of having money work for them. Many people find it difficult to create the assets needed to establish a state of financial independence or a retirement that allows them to live as they lived at the peak of their careers or close to it. Let's look at those possibilities here for a bit.

There are three distinct types of people reading this book.

People who are already financially set, and are now just in it for the game. They may have moved from pursuing financial freedom to using their "wealth" to help other people achieve their goals and dreams.

People who are well on their way to making it happen, but will benefit from some of the ideas here to enhance their existing financial plan. This group as well as the above group may have had setbacks on this journey. There are many former multi-millionaires back at work.

People who don't believe it is possible for them to achieve financial freedom or independence. They feel it is too late for them to start or they just can't see themselves ever getting there. We have some good recommendations for you that may help you change your mind and your reality.

There are a number of things that most financially independent people have in common:

- Many of them own one or more businesses; for example, they are entrepreneurs, or they've established themselves in a profession and managed their funds well. Think about it. Who do you know who is well off? What do they do, or what did they do? Today you can be a business owner in 30 minutes and a successful one in less than 30 months—*one word, Internet!*
- They are often investors, and frequently own cash flow vehicles such as dividend stocks and bonds, mortgages, semi-absentee B Quadrant businesses and real estate.
- They are financially free and have the time and money to enjoy their families and friends on the golf course, or possibly even at their summer home.

Or, they can totally commit to a mission or cause without the difficult challenge of raising money for their projects or their personal support, all according to their value system.

Some do all of the above very effectively. If they are really caring individuals, they also give substantial amounts of their time and resources to charities and/or religious organizations to make the world a better place to live for those less fortunate. Only a compassionate capitalist is a good capitalist in my books. I know entrepreneurs who've given away many times over what they ever kept for themselves. That type of selflessness rates at the top of the list of human beings. We seldom hear their stories.

> Only a compassionate capitalist is a good capitalist in my books.

Chapter 6: Getting All of Your Bucks in a Row

Some people say it happens as soon as you have all your "bucks" in order.

At age 21 I was married with one child and was a very broke schoolteacher. I made $218.00 take-home pay and my net worth was about minus $300. I love summers and I loved to spend time with family on or by the water for as much of the summer as possible. This has always been a big motivator for me. By the time I was 32, our net worth was substantial enough to allow us to spend all of our summers with the family at our summer home in a beautiful country club resort on the lake. I learned at the age of 22 that whatever you can see and believe you can achieve. Another way to put it is if you visualize, verbalize, and actualize, you will realize your dream or your destiny. These concepts are not reserved for the few.

Every ministry, every building, every business, every cause, follows these steps. My dear friend, the late Zig Ziglar, said, "Help as many people achieve their needs and wants, and your needs and wants will be fulfilled to overflowing."

Later, financial freedom for many summers meant spending as much time as possible with friends, our kids and their kids, on our 49-foot yacht, the *Majestic Sanctuary*. For twenty years we played on the gorgeous waters of the Pacific Ocean, amongst the beautiful islands along the Pacific coast of Washington State and British Columbia. Here are a few memorable moments.

- One evening, way up north, snuggled into the glassy waters of Squirrel Cove in Desolation Sound, our granddaughters gave us a concert on the upper deck after dinner just as the sun was slowly setting behind them. The songs came from a musical they had both been in during the previous semester at school. That's just about as good as it gets. All the folks on the yachts around us were on their decks listening in.

- Seeing the broadest grins on our grandsons' faces as they were airborne behind the speeding dingy, as their "young at heart" grandpa was trying to give them the ride of their lives—these times make it all worthwhile. For those of you who have been in that area, we tried to do the "hole in the wall" against the tide as well!

- Sitting high in the Alps holding newborn twins and going skating and skiing with their older brother on awesome memorable trips to Leysin, Switzerland.

- Recently having our two-year-old granddaughter say to me in the parking lot as we were about to leave, "Grandpa, this is an A," as she looked at a license plate. And I ask, "Whose name starts with A?" She said, "Annika" almost before I had asked the question. She keeps walking down behind the cars and says, "Hey Grandpa, I found an L," (for her mom Lisa) and on it went. It was a huge memorable moment for this Grandpa as this little two-year-old was exploding into a whole new world right in front of our eyes!

- Just now to spend two weeks with our youngest family, having the "smartest" two-and-a-half-year-old and our newest darling little grandson.

- To be blessed with four amazing offspring who have terrific spouses is of far more value than getting it all right financially. It has been a blessing to be of help to them along the way as well, as they have now all launched independently into their own worlds.

- To be leaving on a two-week river cruise in Europe in a few days with my wonderful wife of 50 years is something more precious than gold.

We would have missed many of these moments if we were not financially free enough to have been there when they happened. It's not about accumulating things. It's about accumulating experiences and building everlasting memories. But for this to happen, we have to get 'er done, as they say on the Prairies at harvest time.

None of this may be your hot button. You may be wired totally differently, but there must be something that ignites a fire inside of you to be financially free. Our desire is to help you find whatever that is, to move up the timing, or just enhance your existing program a bit by creating a clearer vision of what is possible to achieve as part of your overall destiny.

Security can also be a driving force, as we all know that governments one day soon will be unable to carry the burden necessary to take care of all those who need help. Already only 50 percent pay all of the taxes. The gravy train is quickly running out of gravy, leaving us once again having to take care of ourselves. There is no rocket science or political contriving here, just common sense. When you have fewer people paying into the system because of age and so on, the barrel runs dry. Watch the trends, as we all have a date with another kind of destiny very soon. Better minds than mine will figure it out, I'm sure. In the meantime, do what you can to make life work for you and your family, and for helping others along the way!

Financial freedom begins when your income from your assets exceeds your expenses.

For the purpose of our discussions here, financial freedom begins with having enough money coming in to support the lifestyle you would like to maintain for the rest of your life. Let's use a modest

$100,000, or whatever number works for you, and assume it comes from cash flow investments, retirement programs, and semi-absentee ownership businesses. It is important that this income is somehow linked to inflation.

Now walk through a scenario in the following pages that will clearly help us see how this can be done.

Items we will cover:

1. The basic elements to achieving financial well-being
2. Creating the right mindset
3. Addressing three things that stop you dead in your tracks
4. Putting together a formula for financial independence
5. Establishing a program that leads to financial freedom
6. Creating a solid financial base in the today's economy
7. Cash flow business solutions
8. Action steps

These are the basic elements that take you right to and through the front door to understanding the solutions needed to help you "get there from here."

Section 1

Creating the Right Mindset

If $150,000 or more, in ongoing income, is to be realized, a particular mindset must precede it. It's a mindset where one can readily absorb the reality of this achievement, and one that is completely resolute and positive about making it a reality. For some, this is much easier than others. We'll try to help clear any fog that may dim those prospects for you.

Many folks never establish a clear and focused plan of action to reach a specific goal that relates to their financial independence. Until they do, it never happens. When they do, and when they execute the plan, the results are amazing!

How we think and what we believe is possible have everything to do with where we end up in every area of our lives.

> How we think and what we believe is possible has everything to do with where we end up in every area of our lives.

When the possibility of becoming financially free comes into play, we all arrive on the scene as adults with a particular mindset. It's a mindset shaped by a myriad of influences from parents, teachers and peers, many of them negative. Unless we do major brain surgery on ourselves, we end up exactly where our thinking was on arrival at adulthood.

At age 21 I read the book *Think and Grow Rich.* It literally launched us out of the basement suite where we were surviving on peanut butter and jam sandwiches on the last week of the month, to a monthly income greater than my annual income teaching school, in 10 months. I didn't like the title of the book and struggled with its content at first, but finally realized that it explained the verse that says, "As a man thinketh in his heart so is he!" If, in your heart of hearts, you fear you will become a greedy moneymonger and fall in love with money, you probably already are all of that and will now be able to express it more fully. If you are one who is generous and wanting the world to be a better place, with you being part of the solution instead of part of the problem, that too will be fulfilled.

The basic premise of that book is that you must have an exact written definition of what you want to achieve, and then believe it will become a reality. You do so by finding and working a vehicle or vehicles (jobs, businesses, investments) that take you where you in your heart of hearts want to go. Let not your heart be troubled, but be joy-filled by the good things that are coming your way. There are many good concepts and financial vehicles out there, and a few great ones. Find them.

Right now some of you are drawing a blank and saying you have no clue where to look for something like this. "Faith is the substance of things hoped for, the evidence of things not seen." Believe, and start moving out of Dodge!

There were at least as many baby boomers launched into their financial successes and achievements by Napoleon Hill, Norman Vincent Peale and Clement Stone as by MBA degrees. It was their thinking that changed their world. They adopted a new mindset.

Some of the world changers received their degrees; they just came later, in the form of honorary doctorates because of the causes they so generously supported. Many of their major contributions helped keep the places of learning in business. I have a friend whose foundation contributed over one billion dollars to science. He never had a post-secondary education. He was just an avid reader and lifelong learner and a masterful entrepreneur.

Without taking this step, you are wasting your time going through the other steps, as this first element is the cornerstone to your future financial wellbeing. You can do some mechanical things that work, but believing, visualizing, verbalizing and actualizing adds a dynamic and a creative dimension to the process that gets you there much quicker and easier, while enjoying the ride at the same time because you are inspired to do what you are doing.

> ... believing, visualizing, verbalizing and actualizing adds a dynamic and a creative dimension to the process that gets you there much quicker and easier.

In fact, it's pretty much impossible to be a world changer or even a personal success without "getting" this piece down first—having an open mind towards reaching financial freedom.

The universe or the world around you, or even God himself, doesn't know how to help you until you know exactly what you want. He says He will give you the desires of your heart. When your focus becomes crystal clear and intense, amazing things happen and unusual events begin to come to your aid. Passionate focus brings about amazing results. Only when this has been put to paper, clearly visualized, fervently believed and intensively acted upon, can these objectives be realized. A well-meaning friend visited his cousin on his beautiful well-manicured and successful farm. He said "God has sure blessed you with a beautiful farm." The farmer said "Yes, he surely has, but you should have seen it when he had it all to himself!"

You may say, what about all those dot com millionaires who made it big during the late '90s stock market boom? Many of them certainly didn't have a clear picture of where they would end up. Yes, and that is why most of them ended up back where they started. They didn't have that clear picture that would take them where they wanted to go, so when things got bumpy, it all fell apart for them. There was no clearly determined plan, focus, and determination to sustain them. These fundamental principles were missing from the equation.

There are many aberrations to the above for sure, but overall these principles can be extremely valuable for those wanting to make financial freedom a goal.

A Bit Conflicted Maybe?

Many people are conflicted by what they want financially, and even by what they believe is right for them to want, or by what they think can actually happen for them.

Some people wonder why good things happen for some and not for others. Often the reason for this is that the people who have positive things happen for them totally believe that things will work out for them and that they deserve to win all the time. It is their mindset. When they hit a wall or have a big fall, they just stand tall, brush themselves off and go again.

Often people say when something goes wrong, "I knew that would happen." We regularly get what we expect. It pays to expect good things. Everyone in the end has the same heartaches, setbacks, health issues and traumas as everyone else; they just respond to them differently. There is no escaping the challenges of life. "Problems are the normal state of life," as my late friend Charley Jones used to say.

Creating financial freedom is the same. Few people ever see it happen for them unless they are in sync with the program. I've seen people go from $5,000,000 all the way down to an $80,000 net worth, and eventually to a destitute state in just a few short years. It was primarily because they didn't have the right mindset.

> I've seen people go from $5,000,000 all the way down to an $80,000 net worth, and eventually to a destitute state in just a few short years. It was primarily because they didn't have the right mindset.

The people in question inherited the money and decided they wanted to help others with it, so they gave it all away. Now they themselves are asking for help to survive. Had they invested the five million in a moderate portfolio, it may have grown to as much as 25 million during that same time span and generated over up to 2.5 million every year in return on investment. It would then keep on giving and giving for years to come. Instead it is gone. If you had heard what they were saying you could have predicted the end result. The money was a liability to them rather than an asset.

What comes out of our mouths determines whether we are on the right track or not. I had breakfast with a gentleman some time ago after he attended a creating-wealth seminar the previous evening. He said he hadn't slept much the night before and wanted to create the financial freedom model that was presented. He then proceeded to tell me about all of his financial problems and all of the psychological barriers that were still holding him back from getting there. This happened at each visit.

It is okay to bare your soul to your mentor, but **at some point, you must come to a place where all of your thoughts and words are about the picture you want to create, not the reality you have.** The conversation must begin to totally move towards the plans and strategies that focus you on getting there from here. You can't waste energy and time on the negative of the past or the present because you simply haven't got enough of it to go around. The negative stuff drains you to the point where there are not sufficient brain cells left to focus on the good stuff. Positive and negative thought cannot reside in the same room, at the same time.

> Positive and negative thought cannot reside in the same room, at the same time.

Self-Talk...Watch out!

Self-talk can ruin the whole process. I constantly hear people saying, "It will never happen to me...I will never be financially free." They are so right. It will never happen to them until they change how they think and talk.

What People Say

"Profit is bad"

Many people don't understand that without the profit motive, we wouldn't have an economy. It is ambitious people who love the game that create jobs, invent things, build things, and that take the big risks that make the financial world go round. Some of these people are able to create foundations that efficiently and effectively donate billions of dollars to good causes around the world every year, year after year.

"Money is evil"

Wow, how intelligent is that. A billionaire friend of mine was accosted by a lady one night after a speaking engagement. She said, "Sir, how can you justify owning a jet when thousands of people are starving around the world?"

He said, "I can understand why you might think that, but do you mind if I ask you a few questions?" She said yes. He asked the lady if she thought it was okay for people in Brazil to have a job mining bauxite and for the people there to have jobs driving the trucks that hauled the ore to the ports where it was shipped to the US? She said, well yes. He asked if she'd have any problem thinking it was okay to have job in a smelting plant in the US where they make aluminum out of the bauxite? No. What about the people who work in the plants that manufacture planes out of that aluminum?

She began to get the picture, but he wasn't finished yet. He explained that, in addition to all of the above, he hires a dozen pilots to fly his planes and gives jobs to over 35 people on the ground who take care of the fleet of aircraft. Being able to fly home also helps his executives spend 150 extra nights with their families.

She thanked the gentleman for the new understanding she now had and said she would gladly share it with others.

We all have a tendency to see things through our miniscule viewfinder or the knothole in the fence. Instead, if we are willing to open our minds to what else is going on in the world, it would change not only our perspective, but also our bank balance and our asset-based cash flow.

"I have no interest in money"

This person is either very broke and doesn't mind it, or they're being kept by someone who takes care of their finances for them. Check it out.

"I can't afford it"

Don't be one of those. You're not fun to be around, and for sure, wealth creation is going to elude you big time. So what do you say when you just "can't" afford it? Take the words "I can't afford it" out of your vocabulary if you want to succeed financially.

You may say, it's not expedient at this time, or I need some time to figure out a way to do that before I can give you a definitive answer.

Some say that they can't afford to go to a particular restaurant, that it is way out of their league. Ever just order something from the hors d'oeuvres as part of the menu? Or split an entrée? You can afford the good restaurant. Quit saying "I can't afford it!" It kills your chances of achieving financial freedom. You want to become an "I can afford it" person.

Most people in North America have never been to Europe on a holiday because they think they can't afford it. This is a total falsehood. Almost every year there are airline sales as low as

$450 for a round trip to Europe from North America! Need I say more? It's only a mindset that keeps them from going, plus they could do it on points if they managed their credit cards properly. Life is so small for so many people when it could be so grand if they just took a moment to think about the "possibilities" instead of the impossibilities.

"Investing is risky"

Ah ha... next. No, we will deal with this because it is a legitimate concern that keeps people from moving into the investment arena. If real wealth is to be realized, an element of risk cannot be avoided. The greatest risk, however, is in not becoming an investor.

> If real wealth is to be realized, an element of risk cannot be avoided. The greatest risk, however, is in not becoming an investor.

I once had friend of mine say to me that I wasn't a real businessman because I hadn't lost a million dollars yet. I said, "Gee thanks, but if that's what it takes, I'm not sure if I want to be a real businessman."

Sometime later, I met him in a restaurant and I told him to congratulate me as I'd become a real businessman. He said, "I don't understand." I reminded him of the conversation some years ago. He said, "I didn't say that." Anyway, I informed him that I was real businessman now under his definition. He is still my friend. I have since been invited to a barbecue with him—20 years later and we are all doing fine.

Obviously you don't need to lose a million dollars to make it through the maze to financial freedom, but you have to be brave and go again when it happens, and go again when it happens again, always learning as you go.

If you learn from each experience, the education is priceless. A couple of times I went back and tried the same thing one more time just to make sure it was not the way to go! Not a good thing.

"Money isn't everything"

.. no, but it comes in handy when you get hungry and cold.

Stay away from blaming someone or some circumstance for not getting there.

Never justify your lack of accomplishment and never have victim mentality. People with PLOM (Poor Little Old Me) disease never make it.

Only look to the future with faith and hope in your heart as you make every day count for something good for the future.

Today Is the Day...Always It Is Today

Balanced people say, "Life is more important than money, but money is vitally important for sustaining life—yours, and hopefully thousands of others."

If you learn to have money and assets working for you, you can be free to do the things that are really important to you.

- The time for your kids and other members of your family
- The time to travel with loved ones and friends
- The ability to create jobs and invest in your community
- The ability to help take care of your family's health

- The time to help in your church or do a missions trip yourself
- The time to form a foundation so that hundreds and even thousands of others might live

A key factor that pays big dividends is your ability to give to those who will never be able to take care of themselves.

Joy-filled living comes from joyful giving! Try it, you'll like it!

So to wrap this one up, it's most important to have a clear focus on your endgame. We help you define it here.

The power of the mind God has given us is amazing. It's set up to create and produce almost anything we can get a clear picture of.

You'll recall the story in Chapter 4 about a friend of mine who dreamed of owning a GM motorhome. He found a picture of the vehicle and put it in a prominent place in their home...on the fridge! In the same manner, develop a clear picture of where you want to be in five years financially. Then explore the subject and fill in the blanks as you learn from people much more studied on the subject than I.

It's all the way you think and believe, so go for it now!

Section 2

Releasing Your Brakes

There are several things that keep you from achieving financial freedom. We have just covered a big one. In this chapter, we cover two other entrapments that can keep it all from happening.

Managing Debt

Until one learns to manage debt, or better yet, realizes that for the most part debt is enemy number one, any effort to become financially free is futile. It all begins in high school where credit card companies begin their menacing hold on young people by sending them credit cards in the mail; then the car loan from a relative or friend. Then college or university loans compound the process to the extent that many professionals start their careers with a debt load of over 100 thousand dollars!

> Until one learns to manage debt, or better yet, realizes that for the most part debt is enemy number one, any effort to become financially free is futile.

Someone suggests that two can live cheaper than one and the experiment begins. Lo and behold, it works. A few dollars end up in a savings account and the search for a house begins! One low down payment, and both of the incomes are no longer an option. We are now further enslaved for 30 years or so (a little exaggeration, but you get the point).

The one thing that becomes awkward after a while is using apple crates for chairs. So the Sunday paper comes out with a great ad, "Furniture closeout, nothing down and no payments till June of next year!"

The furniture arrives and a big party ensues, which should really be a wake because of the trauma about to follow and the stress created. As the drama unfolds, the announcement of a little arrival in nine months sends shock waves through a circle of family and friends. One income is impacted for a period of time and additional expenses are added to the already strained budget.

It still happens every day.

Success Can Be Your Enemy!

Your success may complicate and exacerbate the problem we've just described.

Most of you reading this book are fairly upwardly mobile in whatever you are doing, or you certainly have a desire to finish well. So in the next stage, you get promoted and then promoted again, and you get raises and positions and responsibility, and on and on it goes.

Along with success comes the appearance of success and the "Jones" syndrome. With that come the new cars, the bigger home, the vacations, and the debt goes on. Now you have little time to work your investment portfolio, less time for family, and no time for diversity, which is one of the real keys to securing your future.

You can't afford to quit, because you need the money to make it all work. Now you are stuck—and sometimes actually trapped— in a setting that looks so good from the outside but can really keep you from the good stuff that we are about to sit down to hear about.

The Big Thing Here Is Getting out of Debt—All Debt

The first item on the agenda is cutting up a credit card or two and eliminating all high-interest debt. I just got off the phone with a young man who's in the process of getting rid of $65,000.00 of credit card debt! Figure out the monthly payments on that one at 28 percent.

- There are credit card companies who take your debt from another card for 5 percent or less for a period of time just to get your business if you have a decent credit rating. Start there.
- Pay off the cards you have cut up by paying the minimum plus $150 or $200 if possible until it's paid off. We can show you ways to find this money in the next and last chapters.
- Don't charge anything on existing cards that you have active, unless you plan to pay it all off when the credit card bill arrives.
- Do this with each card until they're all paid off. Don't be discouraged by this exercise because you are creating wealth by freeing yourself from making everyone else wealthy except yourself with your hard-earned money.
- When the high-interest debt, like the credit cards and the second mortgage, is paid off, then start on the cars and the first mortgage until it is all gone. Now you can aggressively work on your asset column.

Section 3

How Is Financial Well-Being Created?

Let's talk. Most people think of wealth as making a lot of money, getting a big inheritance, or winning the lottery. None of the above is true. Even though these entities can be contributing factors, they have nothing to do with wealth creation.

We have all seen inheritances blown away overnight and lottery winners who are financially strapped again in 36 months.

> Wealth creation has everything to with developing and managing income and assets. These can eventually create enough cash flow that you can spend your time overseeing the process, and enjoy the rewards of your completed project by becoming a philanthropist.

These investment vehicles at first may just be growth items. They are later converted into other instruments that generate the cash flow you need to live your life as you wish. Or they are cash flow vehicles right from the beginning, such as cash flow real estate or dividend-producing stocks, or semi-absentee-owned businesses.

Another intriguing part of this wealth creation effort is that it has been enhanced by modern technology. Now you are able to develop businesses that have loyal clients purchasing your product or service online by credit card or by bank draft, every month!

When you find a credible business like this or create one, you can speed up the completion of your portfolio by several years.

Section 4

Developing Your Financial Strategy

Now let's start with some common ground by taking a snapshot of someone doing well and on their way to financial freedom. You should be able to develop your own picture from this. Some of you may be way ahead of this snapshot and others some distance behind. It's difficult to presuppose every situation, so here we go.

The most important aspect of navigation is "knowing where you are at all times." Most people think it's "knowing where you are going," which is the second most important thing about navigation.

We are going to carefully look at:

1. Where we are now.
2. Where we want to go.
3. How we can navigate the tricky waters between here and there. It all begins with the money you have available to you from your job, profession or business.

Check out the worksheets on these three items that we've provided for you on our website at www.MyRendezvousWithDestiny. com.

> The most important aspect of navigation is "knowing where you are at all times." Most people think it's "knowing where you are going," which is the second most important thing about navigation.

Chapter 7: Five Key Steps to Financial Freedom

Step One: Cover the Basics

Always have a bread-and-butter plan. I've met many people who have delusions of grandeur about how they are going to become wealthy, and they are out of work. They are looking for the "right position." The right position might be working on construction, digging ditches, or hauling garbage. If one is too proud to do what has to be done to cover the basics, there's no financial freedom up ahead.

> "It is better to get your hands dirty and eat than to be too proud to work—and starve."
> Ancient Proverb

I remember when our youngest son had just finished his Master's degree in religious studies and was working with a construction crew building footings and foundations for homes. He came home covered with mud and with a smile on his face, knowing that he was doing the right thing while he readied himself for his life's work. That New Year's Eve he came home to his beautiful new bride and the beginning of an adventurous life together.

All of our kids have been willing to do that, and I'm extremely proud of them for their willingness to do what has to be done to keep the basics going while they work towards other goals. It's easy to have them as directors and partners in our companies when you know they have that kind of a work ethic and that kind of integrity. They all have it.

The basics are your living expenses: food, clothing, housing, etc.

My brother-in-law is a very successful preacher in a big city church. In between appointments, he doesn't sit around and hope for someone to take care of his "needs"; he paints houses. He's a great painter. He learned the trade while in college and university and is humble enough to use it whenever there's a slack time in his career.

These people are the grist of our society. They win in the end. "He that would be the greatest among you, let him be servant of all." Something many folks never get a handle on and they keep losing as a result.

Always have a contingency plan to make sure you can cover the basics. Get creative, work for free for someone for a week to show them you can do the job, sell stuff on eBay—whatever it takes, do it. Don't suffer, or let your family suffer, just because the "right" thing hasn't shown up. Step one is "always cover the basics."

> "Always have a contingency plan to make sure you can cover the basics. Get creative, work for free for someone for a week to show them you can do the job, sell stuff on eBay—whatever it takes, do it. Don't suffer, or let your family suffer, just because the "right" thing has not shown up.

A young single mom decided she wanted to work for a particular college and she decided she would do whatever she had to just to work there. She was a very well-trained executive assistant with previous experience but didn't like the working conditions. So she applied for a custodial job with the new college. During the interview, the interviewer discovered her talents and told her that the president of the college just lost his assistant. He asked, "Why don't I introduce you to him and see what happens?"

She became an incredible assistant. I know this because the president is my brother-in-law, who told me this story in his office with her sitting just outside. Being willing to do whatever is needed can exalt you.

There's always work available. I don't think I've been out of work for maybe more than two days since I started working summer jobs at the age of 14. If school got out on the 20th of June, I was working no later than the morning of the 22nd. Necessity is the mother of invention. I worked building fences and selling Fuller brushes, and laboured on farms and road construction, for the railroad, in bookstores, for the city making sidewalks, in a service station, and in a saw mill, just to name a few. That was all before I was 20, when I became a teacher and taught for two years before I launched into the distribution business. This morphed into the online shopping business. I always knew that I needed to take care of the basics and did that first!

People say you must have been one of those lucky ones who knew what you wanted to do in life. This is not true. I didn't have a clue. What I did know is that I had to make a living and that having a job was a good start. My dear dad got me into teaching, for which I am most grateful, because I learned to do lesson plans, and communicate with a group and manage a classroom, all of which have helped me immensely when I got into business, did seminars and eventually spoke to thousands of people all over the world.

A job that I liked a lot was road construction. It was real buzz to be sitting high above the ground in the cockpit of a huge earthmover, running at full tilt for a 12-hour shift at 18 years of age. 7 p.m. to 7 a.m.

Being in business was no piece of cake either. Did I do it because I was trained for it, or it was popular thing to do, or it meshed with my personality? No. I did it for the reasons I did every job. First, it paid the bills, and like a lot of work, it seemed to have the possibilities of making our dreams come true as well. Did I eventually get a passion for what I was doing? Yes, of course. When the money was more than we expected, the passion grew even more. Amazing how that works!

> When the money was more than we expected, the passion grew even more. Amazing how that works.

Step Two: Put Your Financial Destiny in Your Hands

Save 10 percent of everything you make. Pay yourself. We pay everybody else. We take care of the auto dealership, the mortgage corporation, the bank, hydro, the finance companies and our credit cards, and so on, but we never write a cheque, or today, transfer funds online into an account named "me" or "ours."

> We pay everybody else. We take care of General Motors, the mortgage corporation, the bank, hydro, the finance companies and our credit cards, and so on, but we never write a cheque, or today, transfer funds online into an account named "me" or "ours."

Where is the invoice from you? It should be paid in the same way that everyone else gets paid. Ten percent. Why 10 percent? Anything less won't get you there from here, and it's easy to figure out. You do it as soon as the cheque comes in. It's the first thing you do. The peace of mind and the freedom it gives you is amazing. First of all, you know you are giving yourself some insurance for the future and you don't feel guilty spending what is designated for that use.

I like to give kids a dollar and ask them how it should be spent. They usually have a bunch of frivolous answers. I tell them that 10 cents goes into savings, 10 cents is given away and the rest can be spent on what they need or want.

Every child who learns that lesson well enough to execute it for their entire life of work is on their way to being more than a millionaire at age 55.

Learning to manage what you have is the key to prosperity. We have a daughter who until recently has shopped for clothes almost exclusively at thrift stores. She is 47 at the writing of this book. She dresses elegantly. The wealthy turn in great stuff to these stores. Some of it has never been worn. It's not about how much you make, but what you do with it, and how you manage what you make, which makes all the difference in the world.

> It's not about how much you make, but what you do with it, and how you manage what you make, which makes all the difference in the world.

Our kids had the privilege of growing up on a beautiful two-acre estate with an indoor swimming pool and lighted tennis court and beautiful landscaping, but we never had a mortgage payment over $450.00 per month. We did have the advantage of a real estate market that kept on moving upwards during an eight-year period, from our first house till the country estate when I was 32 years of age. Most of all, we had the money for substantial down payments because we saved 10 percent of every paycheque. Don't forget that when our oldest son was born we lived in a 650-square-foot basement apartment.

Step Three: Give 10 Percent

This may seem strange as a part of this approach; however, most of those whom I've tried to emulate have this one down. When you plant corn what do you get? When you plant potatoes what do you get? When you give love what do you get? When you sow money what do you get? I know a lot of people have problems with this and I don't blame them, because it sounds really crazy, as if one only gives to get.

> If you plant potatoes you get potatoes, if you plant corn you get corn, if you plant love you get love in return, and if you plant money you will get money in return.

The motivation for acquiring money is the same, whether you trade time for dollars as you do in a job situation, or whether you receive money because you planted it into someone else's life who has a need. It can be explained as one of the laws of God, almost like gravity. I dare you to try it. The problem is that it works so much better if you expect a return on your investment. The worst thing that can happen is that you become a more generous person who cares about the needs of others. It balances you out and helps you become a whole person.

> The motivation for acquiring money is the same, whether you trade time for dollars as you do in a job situation, or whether you receive money because you planted it into someone else's life who has a need.

It all started for me when I went into an insurance office to see the district manager, whom I knew was quite wealthy and had a plaque behind his desk that said, "The secret of living is giving." I read it out loud as I'm sure most people did when they came into his office, and then said, "What does that mean?" He said, "Exactly what it says." I responded with, "That's easy for you to say, you do very well financially."

He asked me if I tithed. I replied, "No, I make $218 a month and if I gave $21.80 we would really be in trouble." He offered to double it if I was short at the end of the month. I said Okay. The following Sunday morning, I put the $21 in the plate at church. I don't fully understand what happened next and I must say it doesn't happen like this for everyone, but we had an incredible month and 40-plus incredible years since.

About the Wednesday after that Sunday I woke up in the middle of the night and was wondering why I wasn't teaching piano, as I was qualified to do that. When opportunity and preparedness meet, exciting things can happen. Then I remembered; we didn't have a piano, and we didn't have room for one either in our 650-square-foot basement suite. Next morning my wife asked me what I had been doing during the night. I told her and she calmly said, "Why don't we rent one?" A few hours later, they delivered our small $10-per-month piano. I already had enough students to pay for the rent plus another $25. We soon had enough to almost double our income.

> When opportunity and preparedness meet, exciting things can happen.

That next week I also went to a car lot and bought a car that needed some serious cosmetic help. I have always been a car buff. I bought it for 50 percent of the asking price with no money down after an hour of haggling.

I took it to a friend's place where we did a number on it. When finished, I pulled into a service station right across the street from where we lived. A gentleman said, "Wow, I love your car! Is it for sale?" I said yes, threw him the keys and suggested he take it for a spin around the block. When he asked me how much, I gave him the dealership's asking price. Three hours later, he and his wife came over with the cheque and the car was gone. I had never made that much money in one lump sum in my life, and that's pretty much how things have gone in that department ever since, as long as we have kept up our end of the bargain. Can I assure you of the same result? No, but there is a principle here that you should experiment with.

Some are quick to say, you should not give to get. If someone can give me one reason why planting and harvesting is any different here than in the other examples I will plead my case. If you have a giving spirit, you give and give some more. If you are a greedy monster, it probably won't work for you anyway, so just bow out. Just having a little fun with you—the principle is a sure one, you are the variable.

Step Four: Find an Opportunity

It's called destiny. You were born with seeds of greatness inside you and there is an opportunity with your name on it. Many of you reading this have found it. You know it is true. If you are still searching, keep searching, but make sure you know what you are looking for. Write it out in detail, including the amount of money, the working conditions, and the freedom and security that it offers.

> You were born with seeds of greatness inside you and there is an opportunity with your name on it.

The biggest problem many people have is a series of mixed emotions. Some of you feel guilty about wanting God's best for you. I can assure you if you are worried that you might become a money monger, you already are one and you might as well have the opportunity to express it. If you think it is the ultimate key to happiness, forget it. It helps, but it takes more than a good opportunity to make one happy. It's an inside job. If you think it isn't fair for you to succeed when others don't and do all they can to keep you in mediocrity, fight these thoughts off and move out to your promised land.

Fulfill your mandate during your stint here. It may be painful. Most of us encounter all the stuff that life can throw at us. But if you're pursuing the dream that has your name on it, you won't notice it quite as much as if you were just muddling through life.

The thing you are meant to be may be far from spectacular. It has to be you, it has to match your energy and ambition levels and be something that gets you out of bed every day with a song in your heart. It could be being a great mom or being a loving, dynamic supporter to your spouse who's on a track to make both of your lives exciting. It could be being the best librarian anyone could ever imagine, or it could be something big and spectacular. "It's gotta be me," as the song goes.

> The thing you are meant to be may be far from spectacular. It has to be you, it has to match your energy and ambition levels and be something that gets you out of bed every day with a song in your heart.

So often people chase someone else's dream, do what they think is impressive to others or do what someone else thinks they should be doing. No. You impress others most when you do what you were meant to do and you do it with all your heart. You do it passionately. Find that opportunity. It's waiting for you. Miracles happen when you step out into the sunlight of walking by faith, to the place that you were destined to be. It may take being humble or it may take realizing you are already there and you are just not leaning into it with passion because of ego or greed. So many people miss what is best for them by searching the world for their opportunity when acres of diamonds are in their own backyard. Trust that quiet inner voice that was put there by your Maker and do the right thing. You then will find the fulfillment you are looking for.

> So many people miss what is best for them by searching the world for their opportunity when acres of diamonds are in their own backyard.

Step Five: Invest

Oh boy, are we having fun yet? This can and has been a roller coaster ride for most people, including me.

"When your income from your assets is greater than your expenses you are financially free"—Robert Kiyosaki. Did he have to say that?

I recommend that you read some good books and follow some folks you feel you can trust not to lead you down the garden path to financial ruin and an ignominious future. A big dark pit awaits investors who place their trust in the hands of greedy self-centred individuals who promise you the moon but are only interested in their commissions or their piece of the action. This can be much more than what is normally considered a commission, if they don't care whether you win or lose.

Let's try to stay positive as we cautiously and briefly approach this subject with care, sensitivity and the understanding that about 80 percent of other folks won't exercise these principles and concepts. They may attempt to keep you from trying them as well.

A
Rendezvous
with
Destiny

After grade 12 and one year of college, I had no idea what I wanted to do with my life vocationally. My dear dad suggested to me one day that I should become a teacher. I had NEVER given that a second thought ever, but it became a big piece of the journey that led to the fulfillment of a destiny.

Chapter 8: Our Story—Putting It All Together

Canadian Prairies to the Board Room—There's Always a Way with Possibility Thinking

"Good evening, Mr. President and Mrs. Reagan. We are Jim and Sharon Janz from Vancouver, Canada. So glad you were able to attend this great event. We have been ardent fans of yours for many years…."

"Oh, hello, Mr. President (Ford)."

"Hey Jim! So glad you are here. Have you met your Prime Minister? Pierre, I was in Vancouver as Jim's guest a few months ago and he put on the classiest function I have been at since I left the White House. It was an amazing event…"

I was born in a small city in southern Saskatchewan in Canada, and lived amidst a small Mennonite community where my dad taught, and where both sets of grandparents as well as uncles and aunts lived. It was still a very primitive part of the world in the early forties.

One of my grandfathers, a part-time minister and farmer, never owned a car. I rode to town with him many times in a horse-drawn carriage called a Bennett Buggy. They had threshing machines, and all the seeding, cultivating and haying was done with horse-drawn equipment.

One year we went for Christmas and did the last 18 miles in a horse-drawn sleigh with hot rocks and horse blankets to keep us from freezing in the bitter cold and blizzard conditions. I never saw tap water or flush toilets until I was eight years old. When I think of what life has been like, I am more convinced than ever that when destiny calls (and it does for almost everyone, if we are listening) the most miraculous things happen if we dare to answer it.

Much of what gets you there is just keeping your act together in all of the above areas, plus being willing to manage your thinking by reading and listening to the right messages, and by believing in the impossible. We'll demonstrate all of this as we press on here.

It's hard to find what you are looking for if you are standing still. You can't steer a ship that isn't in motion. Destiny seldom falls right in front of you. It is discovered. The explorers of old and the space cadets of today dare to venture where no one has gone before.

> It's hard to find what you are looking for if you are standing still. You can't steer a ship that isn't in motion. Destiny seldom falls right in front of you. It is discovered. The explorers of old and the space cadets of today dare to venture where no one has gone before.

Possibility thinking projects you to places you have only dreamed about, and to some you didn't even know existed. If you haven't yet experienced that and you would like to, just hang on and take this ride with me.

Possibility thinking projects you to places you have only dreamed about, and to some you didn't even know existed.

We will tell our story, combining it with what I believe are fundamental truths and principles that made it happen for us, and which I believe can work for anyone who applies them.

Lying in bed one day, I had a dream of a river with products and cans of food floating down the water. Then I saw a small tributary hived off to one side, and it sent these products to me to do business with, by serving people who wanted and needed them. I was about seven or eight at the time. At 21 it happened! The river was brought to me by a great friend.

I must also say that when I was six I bought jaw-breakers from a wholesaler for a penny and sold them for two cents. Something entrepreneurial was stirring within me even then. We moved to Alberta in 1947, where my dad taught in a rather large educational institution in a small town in the middle of nowhere. He had virtually no income, just free lodging and a grocery allowance. There was an "outhouse" in the basement (the mystery crew came once a week to empty it). There was no fridge, just an icebox. There was no running water, just a pump from a cistern in the basement. Life was simple and money was very scarce, so I had to earn my keep during the summers.

I was fortunate never to have to miss a day of work. I started the day after school let out and sometimes worked during the first week of school and got registered for classes as well. Jobs involved stocking shelves in a bookstore, building concrete sidewalks, working on farms, serving on the railway in various capacities, building fences, and working on road construction driving huge earthmovers for two summers. I also worked in a service station and as a tail sawyer in a sawmill one summer way up north. I started working after the *sixth grade* and had many eventful happenings, like overturning one of those earth-movers into a creek.

At age six and seven I used to listen to NHL hockey with my dad on Saturday nights in that little house in Three Hills, and when the Montreal Canadians were introduced by Foster Hewett, I used to skate out onto the imaginary ice in my stocking feet on the linoleum floor, and pretend the crowd was cheering for me.

> …when the Montreal Canadians were introduced by Foster Hewett, I used to skate out onto the imaginary ice in my stocking feet on the linoleum floor, and pretend the crowd was cheering for me.

Fast Forward to the Late 70s

I was having a flashback to those days as we were introduced in that same venue, the Montreal Forum, with ten thousand people cheering us on as we made our way up the stairway to that huge stage to speak. Destiny? You decide.

The willingness to dream big dreams and make many decisions to step out of our comfort zone came many years before this event. Several years after that, sitting at the head table as a founding board member of the Gordie Howe Foundation, I found myself sitting next to none other than the most famous play-by-play hockey announcer ever—the man who I listened to on Saturday nights in that cold Alberta town, Mr. Foster Hewett. It was great to share that story with him. We spent several years very close to Gordie and Colleen Howe, including a cross-Canada speaking tour with them. They are awesome people.

It all really started kicking into gear for me when I was 20 years of age, and I was introduced to the success formulas that caused almost everyone to become successful in that era, even if they would deny ever having read or listened to them. Some people achieved success naturally and some reached outstanding achievements from other angles, but they all used basically the same concepts and principles to get there. I am not one of the "Rich and Famous." I am just an average, ordinary guy who found the right mate, the right concepts, and the right vehicle and was willing to go for it. For me, everything worked out very well.

> I am not one of the "Rich and Famous." I am just an average ordinary guy who found the right mate, the right concepts, and the right vehicle and was willing to go for it. For me, everything worked out very well.

Without a strong work ethic, objectives or dreams, it's tough to find fulfillment and achievement in life. If you don't know where you are going, how do you know when you get there? I feel sorry for people who just cannot find something to stir and motivate their hearts and minds to do something significant with their lives.

By the way—the current theory, that you should only do what you think you are best suited for or what makes you feel good, is bunk. Many times what you are "called" to do or become is totally opposite to that, but in the end it will make a huge difference to those whose lives you touch. Remember, it's not about you, even though it doesn't happen without you being willing to step out, step up to the plate and play ball. Without all the other elements in place there is no game to play.

> Remember, it's not about you, even though it doesn't happen without you being willing to step out, step up to the plate and play ball. Without all the other elements in place there is no game to play.

An insurance man came to our very small basement suite to try to sell this $218-per-month teacher some insurance. After looking at our circumstances, he decided we couldn't even afford a five-dollar-per-month premium. Instead he went out to the car and got a 33-r.p.m. record album called *The Strangest Secret* by Earl Nightingale. I listened to it at least a dozen times in the next few days. I had never heard anything like it! It began to stir something inside of me that, when nurtured and watered by other books and "recordings," started us on a journey that has been nothing short of amazing.

Napoleon Hill came next. Then *The Power of Positive Thinking* by Norman Vincent Peale, *Psycho Cybernetics* by Maxwell Maltz, *The Success System That Never Fails* by Clement Stone, *The Magic of Thinking Big* by David Schwartz, *Move Ahead with Possibility Thinking* by Dr. Robert Schuller, *The Magic of Believing* by Claude Bristol, and *The Secret Kingdom* by Pat Robertson.

Lifelong learning is a vital key to a successful life even if you are a genius, a workaholic, or very skilled with your hands. We have seen recently how several very well-intentioned and highly energized people were suddenly thrust into places of authority and prominence, and due to their lack of knowledge and education in some cases, or their lack of experience and broader understanding in others, they've been embarrassed, or failed miserably while the whole world watched and suffered as well. Their lack of understanding of how the world really works gave way to ultimately disastrous results.

We cannot and are not required to know everything about every discipline for sure, but if we wish to lead broadly, we must have expansive knowledge in many fields, whether that is our specialty or not. Most successful leaders that I know have that broader knowledge of things. Today with the Internet, and with books on every subject, we have no excuse not to know something about just about everything.

Today with the Internet, and with books on every subject, we have no excuse not to know something about just about everything.

Education in itself is a huge discipline and allows one to engage with fellows in all walks of life. It allows us to be part of many communities along the way, which (in most cases) will enrich our lives and allow us to prepare for, and understand better, those who will be part of the fulfillment of our destiny, as it almost always involves leadership. If one is to be a person of influence, one must be a person of broad understanding and vast knowledge. Read, read, read and tune in to all kinds of media. Just never quit learning your entire life, formally and privately. It will help you with your calling and in your ability to touch others while (one hopes) aging much less quickly!

> Just never quit learning your entire life, formally and privately. It will help you with your calling and in your ability to touch others while (one hopes) aging much less quickly!

Living below the Poverty Line

At 21, I suddenly found myself with offers to join an insurance company, an auto dealership and a plethora of direct marketing companies. I wasn't ready for this. I was a very broke teacher. When my wife came home with our first baby, she asked me to get a bottle warmer worth $1.98, but I only had $.50 in my pocket and the bottle warmer had to wait. I know what it is like to be living below the poverty line. That was one of the lower moments in my life.

Seven months later, I resigned my teaching job in hopes that my fledgling marketing venture would get enough momentum for me not to have to return to the classroom in the fall. I was young and stupid, but in August, during one of the toughest months in the industry, we did amazing things. For the first time we began to realize how powerful the concepts I had read and listened to over the past nine months had been.

We had a crystal clear goal and gave total attention and focus to it, and it was effective. We believed that our goal would become a reality even though there was little to substantiate that it could be achieved in that short space of time. We made about $1,500 that month (the average wage in 1964 was about $450) and as we flew over Winnipeg at 42,000 feet, two weeks later, on an all-expenses-paid trip to our head office, my lovely wife, who up till this point had just been hanging on for dear life, said, "This is really real, isn't it?"

Whatever you can see and believe, and can passionately act upon, you can achieve. We experienced for the first time what it means when it says, "Faith is the substance…of things hoped for even when you can't see it up ahead." When you visualize, verbalize, and actualize you are always on your way to achievement.

> When you visualize, verbalize and actualize you are always on your way to achievement.

I have enjoyed cars ever since I was a little boy. I drove anything I got a chance to drive from a very early age. At 17, I found myself perched many feet above the ground on a huge earthmover from 7:00 at night until 7:00 in the morning, six days a week and for several summers. Vehicles of all kinds grabbed my attention. When I was 18 my friend and I did a motor job on a 1953 Ford during my first year of college. It was a great car.

I bought a new 1964 Chevy Impala hardtop, and 10 months later the '65s came out. The new style was awesome. I hinted to my wife that it might be time to trade. Well, you can imagine how that went over. We now lived in a nice three-bedroom rented home with a full basement that I had made work in order to run our business. Not wanting to spend money on a rented house, I cardboarded over the studs and covered them with a brick-and-vine-patterned wallpaper. After the wet paper dried, it left a real lifelike texture!

Our business was doing very well and we were now making almost 10 times the average wage, so I asked my wife, "If I double the business this month from the previous several months' average, may I buy the car? Please?" She did a quick calculation, realized it was impossible to do, and said, "Of course!"

I went into that basement "office" and sat down at my "executive" desk, which was made up of a door set upon two other furniture items that somehow worked. I swept everything off the desk into the huge garbage can right beside it and said, "If it is important enough, they'll write back," and proceeded to tape paper over the entire desk where I began to diagram our entire organisation with projected numbers for the month. When I finished I was $10,000 short, so I decided I would have to create $10,000 in new business with people who were not yet involved.

Warning: Please Do Not Do the Following—It May Ruin Your Reputation for Good!

Fresh out of prospects, I went to the yellow pages. Unfortunately, it was 3 a.m. when I began to phone for appointments, because the clock was ticking and it was already the third of the month. I called owners of shops I'd been in and had made some connection with, who had published their home phone numbers in the book. You get funny reactions when you phone people at 3 a.m. People awakened from sleep are usually not in the best mood and they are sure something very traumatic must have happened, especially if grandma hasn't been well.

You get funny reactions when you phone people at 3 a.m. People awakened from sleep are usually not in the best mood and they are sure something very traumatic must have happened, especially if grandma hasn't been well.

I explained to them, "You probably don't know me and after me calling at such a ridiculous hour you probably don't ever want to know me, but I have something urgent I need to see you about tomorrow and I won't have time to call later. Would 10 a.m. at the coffee shop next to your place be okay?" I called until I had an appointment every hour from 7 a.m. till 5 p.m. People showed up just to see if my phone call was a nightmare or if this nutcase was real. It was one of the most productive days of my career. Out of that day and the next two I brought in enough business to accomplish my goal by the end of the month. I was actually $45 short, but I bought the car anyway—with cash.

Please heed the above warning, this is not recommended!

I picked the car up at noon and drove to a city over 300 miles away for a meeting that night. I broke the car in at just over 100 miles per hour all the way. Youthful, 23-year-old craziness. It never wanted to go slower after that!

If you can see, believe and passionately act on your goal, you can and you will achieve it!

Now for the Big Event!

We are in Jamaica. It is the first day of a two-week all-expenses-paid trip in a beautiful oceanside suite. A man brought a book to the event, *Become a Possibility Thinker Now!* by Robert Schuller. "*No, no, no!*" I revolted, "I need a vacation!" But up to the suite we went with some friends of ours and began to dig into the message of this book.

"If you believe all things are possible"… okay!

We considered this for several hours and when everyone left I asked my wife what she'd been thinking about in regards to our goals during our three-hour discussion. She said, "You go first." I said, "Does it start with a T?" That was the first letter of our next award level in the business. She said, "No." I said, "Does it start with C?" This was another, much higher, award level in the business. She said, "Yes!" I said, "I've been thinking about that, too."

That short conversation changed our lives and thousands of other people's lives over the next many years. It is still in play to this day as we share the story I am about to tell you now.

C stands for Crown, which was the highest award available at the time.

This Is Intense

Here's an abbreviated version of what happened in the next 15 days.

We booked a flight to go home the next day, leaving a two-week all-expenses-paid trip behind only to land in Toronto, Canada, in a blizzard and minus-30-degree weather, at 3 p.m. November 15, 1972. We went to the Constellation Hotel where we had stayed many times before, and were sure we could get a room there mid-week. We were wrong. They were totally full. (By the way, they just demolished that hotel a few months ago.)

My wife was six months pregnant at the time and very tired. I said to the hotel manager, "You must have something." They explained they had a sample room that is used by business people to show their wares. "It has a Murphy bed in it." I said, "Let's take a look." As we approached the door I noticed a brass plaque on the door. It said, "THE CROWN ROOM!" I said, "We'll take it!" Destiny? You decide.

Three-hundred-and-fifty dollars' worth of phone calls occurred that night to inspire the troops for the ride of their lives. We basically had to double the base of our business, which was already doing extremely well, in 15 days.

> Three-hundred-and-fifty dollars' worth of phone calls occurred that night to inspire the troops for the ride of their lives. We basically had to double the base of our business, which was already doing extremely well, in 15 days.

A Total and Absolute Impossibility

It had never been done before and, as far as I know, has never been done in North America since. I stopped in Winnipeg to work with one group, then Calgary to work with number two and three, then Edmonton and on to Vancouver for the balance. I hardly slept, working 19-to-20-hour days flat out with my colleagues, to attempt the impossible.

When there was 48 hours to go, I received an early call from one of the participants. He said, "Faith is the substance," and hung up. Think about that statement. All 10 marketers were short about $2,500 each with 48 hours to go. There was only one thing left to do and that was to have faith that somehow, some way, $25,000 to $30,000 worth of business would materialize from somewhere with this exhausted and totally depleted crew.

It's the last day, November 30th , and the temperature is -30 again. I'm in Calgary visiting with group #9 at lunchtime. He was still $2,500 short. He is feeling very badly that he would be the spoilsport in this deal. I said no: from the Crown Room in Toronto 15 days ago until now, only miracles have happened. We have four hours left till the warehouse closes. It will happen.

It's 4:00 p.m. I'm at the warehouse in Calgary and a white station wagon slides to a stop in the snow in front of the building. My lunch buddy was waving an order from some folks way up north for about half of what he needed. I asked, "Why are you so excited about this?" He said, "Come inside and let me tell you the rest of the story."

He went on to tell me how a couple of older ladies in Toronto in his group had a fundraising evening for a missionary priest friend of theirs two day ago. They did twice what was needed to meet his target! I just looked up in that driving snow and did what so many athletes do when they score that winning goal. I said, *"Thank you!"*

Thumbnail Sketch

This has obviously been a thumbnail sketch of what happened during those crazy 15 days. But it's an amazing demonstration of how faith works. If you believe, all things are possible. "With man it is impossible, but with God all things are possible." You might say, "Oh, there is a lot of stuff in between those words you have just quoted." Yes, you are right, and we are not going to do a theological thesis here for sure. I'm just telling you that, for me, this kind of faith-filled focus worked out well on numerous occasions, as it has for many other people I know. Plus "the rain falls on the just and the unjust". More for you to ponder.

"With man it is impossible, but with God all things are possible."

Chapter 9: Ten Ways to Work Smarter Rather than Harder

Here are 10 ways to get there from here—10 ways to work smarter in a business setting.

1. Seldom do for others what they are capable of doing for themselves.

For years, I've done business previews and have taught people how to do them. Few people ever think they are ready to do one themselves. I usually only got them to do it the way an eagle gets its eaglets out of the nest; she pushes them out when she thinks it's time.

I had a young eager-beaver attending my sessions with up to 20 people in attendance. He was not going to do one on his own so I set one up at his house. He invited the world. I dropped some materials, a white board and an easel off at his place in the afternoon, with the excuse that I didn't want to wait until the last minute to show up with all this paraphernalia.

From his house I went to the airport, as I had meeting in another city that night. I called him at 7:30. He said in hoarse voice, "Where are you?" I told him, and said, "Goodbye Ray, and have a good meeting." He had nine prospective candidates there, along with 12 other folks in the business. He did a horrible job. He had people up at the board helping him. The meeting lasted until 1:00 a.m. However, all of the nine candidates registered for the business and I never did another meeting for him. Many millions of dollars of business and 38 years later, that business is still producing a profit. (By the way, I had lunch with him the day before that meeting, and had him go through the presentation, so I knew he was mentally ready. He just needed to get over the jitters, and so on.)

I could tell you stories like this all day and night. This is tough to do, but if you don't learn to do it, you are always limited by your own 15 hours of production a day instead of, at times, possibly a thousand or more. That's 15,000 hours of productivity in your arena of influence every day. On a domestic level, it's like getting the kids to wash their own clothes, clean their own rooms, and so on. The lesson is this: either delegate, or stagnate.

The most amazing example of building a mammoth business by letting leadership and success-driven people maximize their talents and abilities through the free enterprise system was started by two young Dutch fellows. They'd failed at almost everything they'd done until they became distributors for a rather small vitamin company called Nutrilite. In short, along with a few other members of their team, they decided to start their own sales business by forming an organization called the American Way Association.

The Association was designed to look for products to sell through their unique (at that time), multi-level marketing plan designed by a marketing firm called Midingger and Cassleberry. Rich DeVos and Jay Van Andel were selected to head the entire venture. That small band of ambitious leaders became the foundation of an organization that's grown to over 3 million strong and almost 12 billion dollars in global sales! DeVos and Van Andel just fed and managed the monster as it grew, and it grew to a large extent on its own, for over 50 years. We know it today as Amway. Van Andel gave a famous talk at one of their huge conventions entitled, "Delegate or Stagnate!" They certainly had that wired. I was privileged to speak at that same convention.

Although the company has weathered some big storms, their basic integrity and sound business principles brought them into a whole new and exciting era of growth and development as they evolved into one of the biggest online shopping companies in the world, driven by several million independent business owners.

2. Keep a balance on everything you do — family, personal, social, financial, vocational, and spiritual.

We are people of extremes. When we overdo it in one area, another suffers. If we do this long enough, something breaks and then all the extra effort that we put into our "spiritual life," for example, goes down the drain when our spouse leaves us, we have to declare bankruptcy, or our kids turn out to be less than they could be. It's not easy but investing our time in a balanced fashion pays big dividends in the end.

Do what's right in every area of your life. That is way tougher than it sounds. I try but do I ever fail a lot. I take comfort in John Maxwell's concept of failing forward.

These six areas are like spokes in a wheel. All we have to do is lose one and the wheel wobbles.

We find this in our business ventures, where people take a new idea and make it *the* focus instead of just adding it to the existing business as an enhancement. Lopsided stuff always topples over sooner or later.

3. Do "only" goal-oriented activities.

Keep focused on where you really want to end up because you will always end up in the direction of your gaze.

Keep focused on where you really want to end up because you will always end up in the direction of your gaze.

I landed in Lansing, Michigan, in a blinding snowstorm one afternoon. Our connecting flight was cancelled, and the airline lined up a bus to take us to Grand Rapids. The lady bus driver was scared to death driving in this mess and kept looking at the ditch through the right front door of the bus. Guess where we ended up? (No slight on lady bus drivers. I've had some very good ones). This is when you say you've had "one of those days"!

Do the tough stuff first every day

Do the productive stuff, the kind of things that produce income for the company and/or yourself first. Make up your to-do list and put an "A" beside all the truly goal-oriented activities. Get onto those before you get caught fiddling around on your computer or answering emails that have nothing to do with your bottom line or where you're going.

One of the hardest things to learn is that business is about numbers

If the numbers are not in the right column more days than not, you will be out of business soon. If you're not making more money for your company than they are paying you, why are you there? Now there's a thought. Do an inventory every week to see what you have contributed to the bottom line.

The company's goal has to be your goal

If it is not, you shouldn't be there. If you don't think you are being paid what you are worth, start your own business and find out what you are worth. Or figure out how much you contribute to the bottom line of the company you work for. Remember, it costs the company at least twice what you are making to break even. The space you take, the expenses you create, the taxes and benefits they pay, it goes on and on.

You can't get there from here if you don't do at least five goal-oriented "A list" activities a day. Remember to do them first each day, whenever possible.

4. Periodically step back and look at the picture you are painting

Step back and look to see if it's turning out the way you had imagined. In this case, the picture is your life. Artists do that every hour or more. We should do it at least once a week. Is what you are doing effectively getting you where you want to go? Take a day off just to check and reflect. It helps you stay on track and refresh your memory as to why you are doing what you are doing. Keeping a clear picture of your destination helps you get there from here so much sooner, and so much more efficiently.

Our subconscious works better than our conscious mind. That may sound like heresy, but for me, and the hundreds of the successful I know, it was their constant and clear understanding of the big picture that got them there. Being buried in the details and in the "work" soon causes you to lose your way. Make sure you understand your "why" is bigger that your "but"!

Being buried in the details and in the "work" soon causes you to lose your way. Make sure you understand your "why" is bigger that your "but"!

5. Utilize everything that's going on to maximize every move you are making.

Often our ego gets in the way of this one, too. Plan your moves—I mean your physical moves—like traveling around the city, around the country and the world. Always check to see what you can plug into that can help you get where you are going. It may be a seminar for yourself or your people. By the way, you may have noticed that you can't achieve too much success by yourself.

The world and the Internet is full of people and ideas to help you get where you want to go. Tons of free stuff is waiting at your fingertips. You can do a meeting on Skype or a myriad of other media programs that allow you to talk to people across town or around the world without getting in your car, looking for a parking place or flying anywhere. There's no telling how far you can get if you don't care who gets the credit!…and it's free.

> There's no telling how far you can get if you don't care who gets the credit!…and it's free.

My son-in-law, who lives in Indonesia at the moment, hired all of his new staff from around the world this year, doing the interviews on Skype. He saved the school of which he is principal over $60,000 dollars in airfares and hotel rooms, let alone the wear and tear on the body. I just did a quick online meeting face to face with someone 1,000 miles away a few minutes ago, between the last paragraph and this one, on this computer. It could turn into a substantial profit for my associate who needed assistance closing a product sale. The buyer was impressed that we could connect this way and give that kind of customer service. Use technology, use functions, use audiovisuals, use the Internet, and grab every book and resource that fits into where you are going.

6. Stay rested and in shape.

This is my Achilles heel. I've done a poor job of both over the last many years. Balance is the key. Being a Type A, when I get into a project, like writing a book, I just love to get unbalanced and throw everything into getting it done. I often have an excuse for missing the 30 minutes on the treadmill, or ordering the wrong thing for dinner or lunch. Having travelled almost half of my life, and being on the banquet circuit, could be an excuse, but then my friend Zig Ziglar blows that one all to heck.

While in the hospital with a heart incident, my wife and my son came to see me. I ignorantly asked, "What does ICU stand for?" When I found out, I said, "Oh gads, then this must be serious." My first morning in there, I set up shop by using the cart table they use for meals as my desk, and my cell phone was working beautifully. I heard one of the nurses say, "What is he doing in there?" She said, "I think he's running the world from there."

I heard one of the nurses say, "What is he doing in there?" She said, "I think he's running the world from there."

Shortly after that, I guess one of my electrode thingies came off, sending one of the nurses flying into the room. Without stopping, she dove under my gown to check on me. I was on a long-distance call and had to tell my friend that I needed to call him back because a nurse had crawled up my blue thing and she was asking me to hang up.

The night before, when I came into emergency, I was joking around with the attending nurses and doctor, when one of the nurses said, as she briskly walked away, "Oh, I know your type; one minute you're joking around and the next minute, you're gone." I said, "Thank you for that, Miss. That's called bedside manners."

Anyway, I say all of this to show it's my weakest area. We all have one or two weak areas, given to us so we can all sing that wonderful spiritual, "Amazing Grace," and mean it. We all need grace.

7. Build on your strengths, not only your weaknesses.

To get there from here in one lifetime, you can't be superman or woman, nor can you be all things to all people. Find out what you're good at and get better at it. You'll find that you may even improve in some of your lesser gifts. Don't let your well-meaning spouse, friend or even mentor try to focus all your attention on your weakest areas.

There are thousands of sessions going on around the country and world every day for people who need help in their weakest areas. I laud those sessions, like the 12-step programs and others like it. But when did you last hear about a session to help you build on your strengths? Not too often. The problem with so many folks is that they spend every waking hour worrying and fussing over their deficiencies rather than moving on with their assets and abilities.

> The problem with so many folks is that they spend every waking hour worrying and fussing over their deficiencies rather than moving on with their assets and abilities.

I've seen people who never get to the other side of their issues. Addictions I understand, but your feelings about your father or a former spouse, or even you own past shortcomings, need to be forgiven and forgotten if you want your future to be better than your past. Easier said than done? Of course, but it doesn't change the fact that a great future depends a lot on a forgiven and forgotten past. Grace is greater than all of our shortcomings of the past, and it is available to you for free.

A great future depends a lot on a forgiven and forgotten past. Grace is greater than all of our shortcomings of the past, and it is available to you for free.

8. Delegate or don't do C activities often if you want to get there from here.

Some of the most important people in the world are support people. It's a role that some people have chosen, and without these people, the world would come to a grinding halt. I saw the most excellent example of this the other day while watching an NHL hockey game. One of our fastest and best players broke his stick. The very alert stick boy grabbed one of his sticks and had it in the player's hands in less than 5 seconds. The player grabbed his stick, took a pass from centre, and two seconds later scored the winning goal. The hockey player got the roar of the crowd but the stick boy won the game as well.

Some people would say that's not fair. Baloney. It's a choice, and that stick boy is thrilled to be helping the best athletes in the world perform at their best. By the way, that stick boy is a professional at what he does and has been doing it for the same team for 28 years. He's also a great high school teacher that taught my kids.

No pit crew, no race. No race car and driver, no owner, no pit crew necessary.

There are so many unsung heroes in the world. I love these people. It's the lock-and-key principle: one is not worth more than the other, and one is useless without the other. To be a good support person, you have to be humble enough to take instructions and take them quickly and efficiently, willingly and happily. That stick boy came over the boards with his arms in

107

the air when that goal was scored! He'd done his job in all the ways I just described.

So remember to delegate C activities. If you're a visionary, a leader or a business owner, you must keep the main thing the main thing, and allow others to help you make that big picture become a reality. When you're in the hunt, you may not have time to mow the lawn or go to the bank. It usually takes a team to make something big happen.

> If you're a visionary, a leader or a business owner, you must keep the main thing the main thing, and allow others to help you make that big picture become a reality.

9. Make sure you have your subconscious computer working for you 24/7.

Your mind is ready and willing if you just commit to it. God has endowed us with a mechanism that's most amazing and quite unexplainable. Years ago I read Maxwell Maltz's *Psycho-Cybernetics* and it changed how I went about making things happen. Things got a lot easier. Joseph, of Biblical times, had a dream that he never lost sight of even though he was sold into slavery and imprisoned twice. He punched that picture so firmly into his subconscious through faith that he ended up the ruler of the richest nation on earth at the time. Along the way, he also always did what was right, never flinching in his commitment to following his conscience.

Basically it has to do with taking your goals, objectives and the places that you want to get to from here, and giving them by faith to your subconscious and to God to work on. It's the biggest part of your mind, like an iceberg under the water line, and is very capable of helping you get there in a timely fashion.

Have you ever said, "I can't believe this! It has happened exactly the way I imagined it!" Start believing it and imagining it on purpose. We as human beings are fearfully and wonderfully made and have far greater potential than we know.

> We as human beings are fearfully and wonderfully made and have far greater potential than we know.

Most Olympic athletes say that when they stand on the podium, they have dreamed of and visualized that day since they were very young. The hard work was necessary, but without the dream the work would not have taken place, and the deed would be left unaccomplished. Their purpose (their why) was bigger by far than their excuses (or buts).

10. Consciously bathe all of your activities in a positive attitude.

We know it's all about attitude. Our reaction to our circumstances is what it is all about. Most of the time, our circumstances stink.

My dear recently departed friend, Charley Jones, used to say, problems are the normal state of life and the only ones who don't have any, are where he is now. He would call me at any hour of the day or night, like 3 a.m., and say, "Hi, tremendous Jim, how are you doing?" I would ask how he was doing and he'd say, "I'm so tired of being happy, so don't give me any good news." He would say this when he was battling cancer and other serious difficulties, and he meant it. He lit up the lives of millions in his 80 years. He lived his last years in the valley of the shadow of death. He did it without fear and with an amazingly positive attitude.

The longer we linger in the valley of negativity, pity, and self-doubt, the longer it takes to make a difference in other people's lives. Charley used to say that many people have PLOM disease—Poor little old me.

It's good to do attitude checks many times a day. Take the project you are working on now and make sure you are coming at it from a positive perspective. What a difference it makes! It definitely helps you get there from here!

There you have it, 10 ways to work smarter, not necessarily harder unless you want to. These ways reduce your effort index and help you accomplish more in less time!

Chapter 10: Stay the Course—Rabbit Trips Are Calling at Every Corner

The course is the trajectory of your destiny. You are ready to go, once you've discovered or chosen it, and you know where you are, and where your next port of call is; your charts, your planned and plotted compass headings have been spelled out, and your instruments are functioning properly.

It's a Saturday morning at the Semiahmoo Resort in Blaine, Washington. We've just completed a leadership seminar. A few "stay behinds" are on board our yacht as we head across Georgia Straight, over to the beautiful island of Sucia in the San Juan Islands for the day. It's foggy and the horizon is not visible, but being the optimistic captain that I am, I assured our guests that the fog would soon burn off and visibility would return.

Visibility is not zero, but it's not good. Gloria Askew, author of a best-selling book called *The Secrets of Supplements*, comes up to the bridge and says in her typical inquisitive way, "How do you know where you are going, Jim? All we can see is water and fog."

I showed her my chart and how the compass heading led to a marker that would appear on our port side some 35 minutes straight ahead. I explained that once we reached that marker we would make a 27-degree course correction for seven minutes to port in order to avoid a rocky reef, then make a hard right into the beautiful bays on the island of Sucia. The radar is also helpful to keep from colliding with other vessels that may be out in the straits on this rather foggy morning. Just in case you wondered, due to my age, the charts were on my laptop and my GPS was speaking out, showing our location brilliantly and clearly.

Gloria, noticing the depth sounder showing 357 feet, and not being shy about asking questions if her life may depend on it, says, "How do you know all this?" I told her I took a course and I mostly learned it from experienced boating mentors. She asked, "How do you know you'll get to that spot?" I said, "I trust those who taught me. I trust the charts. I trust my compass, and my GPS. All of this is necessary to keep me on course. I also trust my 'see-in-the-dark instrument,' my radar. Above all now, I trust my experience of many hundreds of hours of navigating these waters."

If I'd looked at the shadows out there or decided to go on my own instincts, we could have ended up on the rocks that day. Instead, by staying the course, 35 minutes later the marker showed up 20 feet off to our port side, the fog had lifted, and the amazing Island of Sucia was looming up ahead.

We all have mentors who've gone before us. I have had inexperienced people grab the rudder and say, "Why don't we go here!" Not good! One must know what they are doing when they venture out into new territory.

We were in Winter Cove in the Gulf Islands one beautiful Sunday afternoon when some young guys came up to us in their 18-foot boat and asked, "Where is Cabbage Island?" I asked them for charts to show them. They said, "Charts? What are charts?" They actually had a road map! These guys were very lucky to be alive as they were in a very precarious area with rocks and shoals everywhere.

We all need to learn the system we are operating in, whether it is boating, flying, education or business. If a functioning entity does not have a system, it's doomed to fail. Most of us have all the tools available to us to guide us safely to our place of destiny. All we have to do is take the time to learn how to use them.

Let me be an encouragement to you today while helping you with some guidelines to *stay the course*. None of us will stay the course if that is our only goal. It takes a lot more than that to keep us doing what we need to do to take us to the finish line.

> None of us will stay the course if that is our only goal. It takes a lot more than that to keep us doing what we need to do to take us to the finish line.

It's a tough world out there with tons of distractions. It's a world of NOISE and dissension, cynicism, hate and mistrust. It's a world of tensions, dysfunction and stress, and we have trouble at times staying focused on what it is all about in the midst of this turmoil. We must focus if we are to succeed.

Those of us who belong to organizations and businesses that encourage reading inspirational books, listening to CDs, and attending seminars are fortunate to live in a world of optimism, friendship, love, appreciation and trust. These are novel concepts in a world that hardly believes that is possible anymore, even in some churches.

We, who aspire to succeed and know that we can do something about it, have so many things going for us. If you're reading this now, you are probably one of those privileged few who have found your purpose or your dream and are seriously wanting to fulfill your destiny. If not, keep looking for it. If it's a business you want, look for a dynamic B Quadrant business opportunity that has unique, outstanding products or services. You also want to make sure it's supported by an effective and electrifying personal and business development system, one that trains, teaches and motivates by pulling the very best out of all who commit to doing what the venture espouses and calls for.

Organizations like this are an oasis for the restless and the unfulfilled, a vehicle for those wanting to achieve more, and a source of knowledge for those desiring to know how to get there from here.

However, only when we know exactly why we want to achieve, will we ever be able to take that knowledge and desire and make it a reality. Only then will things happen beyond our wildest dreams. Without that specific reason or purpose that makes us want to get out of bed in the morning, nothing of lasting significance happens.

> Without that specific reason or purpose that makes us want to get out of bed in the morning, nothing of lasting significance happens.

We need to find that *God-given dream*, a destiny that's been planted inside all of us before we were even born—some believe even before the foundations of the earth were formed. Without this, we are stuck with something less than the best for our lives. Find it and begin to make it a reality. Only then does personal fulfillment begin. Your dream may not be your vocation. Think about that.

In Bruce Wilkinson's book *The Dream Giver* he says, "Everybody was made to be a somebody and the key is to wake up the Big Dream that God has planted inside of us and then set out on a journey to achieve it." Bruce takes us through the steps necessary to work this process of finding and achieving that unique purpose for which we are placed here for a while— a process that all the great dreamers in history have gone through.

Here are the steps.

1. Become aware of your personal destiny. Don't fret or panic, just keep moving, trusting it will show up as you become more aware of good opportunities.
2. Face the fear and leave the place of comfort. Your future is not here.
3. Be prepared to encounter massive opposition from those around you.
4. Get ready to work through a period of difficulty that tests your belief in your dream.
5. Learn to surrender to the call and, by faith, stay the course.
6. Conquer the huge obstacles that stand between you and the fulfillment of your dream.
7. And finally, you will reach your full stride and your potential when you begin to achieve all that you were meant to become and accomplish.

There are many hurdles to overcome. Winners use those hurdles to build strength by making them just another breakthrough experience that propels them to the next big event on the journey. Bruce goes on to say that, "Only you can discover the dream that will give you true fulfillment and cause you to be all that you were created to be."

As we pursue that dream, the empty places in our lives begin to fill in, and only as we become knowledgeable about who we are and why we are doing what we are doing, can we effectively reach out to help others fulfill their purpose in life.

As we pursue that dream, the empty places in our lives begin to fill in, and only as we become knowledgeable about who we are and why we are doing what we are doing, can we effectively reach out to help others fulfill their purpose in life.

Fulfilling Our Purpose in Life

I want to speak to those of you who've had an intense dream; those of you who think you know what your dream is and those of you who don't have a clue what your dream is.

First to the clueless:

Listen to your heart. What gets your attention? When do you really enjoy yourself? Is it a particular lifestyle? Is it the financial freedom that can allow you to do what you really want to do? Is it a cause much bigger than yourself and your lifestyle? Mother Teresa set such an unparalleled example of what that was all about.

Success in business, creating wealth or any other fulfillment of a dream should not be an end in itself. It may be the toughest thing you ever did, but for most of you, it is the vehicle to take you to be fulfilled in those areas of life that really matter.

Many people are living lives of quiet desperation, full of hurts and financial stress. Only when you know why you are doing it and only when your desire to achieve it exceeds your trepidations, are you ready to ignore the noes and the fears that we all suffer.

People with the passion to achieve their dreams have done amazing things. They've paid the price. I've spent much time with Dr. Schuller, and from the time his uncle said to him at eight years of age, "Robert, you are going to be a great preacher someday," the destiny was set. Was it all a bed of roses? Oh no! Many traumas followed, starting a church in a drive-in theatre. Knocking on 3,000 doors several times to introduce himself to the neighbourhood and invite them to try out the unique church in the drive-in. Accidents and health problems almost claimed his, his daughters' and his wife's lives; he endured financial stress that most of us would cave under, and so on. Now, like so many other "greats," he suffers the indignity of deep challenges in the organizations he built for so many years. It hasn't changed the fact that millions of people were helped and inspired by this man. We dare not critique, as our days are not yet finished.

Many of us are so wimpy. Our society has taught us never to deny ourselves or to suffer pain of any kind; so many turn to various drugs to dull the hurt or help them forget. This has left us with a disproportionate number of people who are getting left behind, never to fulfill their God-given potential.

Bruce Wilkinson

Bruce Wilkinson says, "Let me encourage you. Never think that since you are struggling, you are a secondclass Dreamer; just remember that there is no way for any of us to reach our dreams without leaving our recliners...over and over again. We love the recliner...it is our escape from what we know we have to do to really become a consistent home run hitter. It's what we do before 7:00 a.m. and after five that turns ordinary people into those who do great things."

A man named Kenton from Kenya had this to say, "I have broken through my comfort zone in key areas of my life, but I keep finding new areas that I have to deal with if I want to live my Dream." He then asks, "Does the discomfort ever go away?"

Tyler Saxton

I heard a television interview last week of a young man by the name of Tyler Saxton. He was born as an unwanted child. He was three months premature, and when his mother saw him for the first time, several days after his birth, she broke into tears. He had two collapsed lungs. Tubes were coming out of him everywhere. He was black and blue all over his little body. He was diagnosed with Cerebral Palsy. They said he would never walk, he would probably be blind, and he would be mentally disabled. What a future.

His mom said from early childhood he seemed to have a determination to live and to live fully. He had numerous operations, including that of cross-wiring his back so that he could stand and walk erect. Today he is 18, in grade 12 in high school. He scuba dives, plays golf and has written a book. He also speaks several times a month at youth events to encourage kids that they can fulfill their dreams in whatever type of circumstance they find themselves. As he stood there tall and handsome last Sunday, in front of 4,000 people and 10 million television viewers, he let the listeners know that the decision to stay the course and win was in their hands.

Sun Ki

We have an associate who, in 13 months, built an amazing block of business. It's a business that will be the foundation of a long-time business venture. His dream is to use his business model to spread goodwill around the world. That is his passion. He shared that message with emotion and passion at a leadership function the other day.

We had lunch with him last week and he shared how he stays the course. He does three business presentations every single day, six days a week, and does three training sessions every week as well. That is in cement. He just does them every week without fail.

Sun Ki told us that for him, believing that he'll win is the biggest part of staying the course and reaching his destiny.

> Sun Ki told us that for him, believing that he'll win is the biggest part of staying the course and reaching his destiny.

Gordie Howe

A few years ago, we had the privilege of meeting and spending a lot of time with the great hockey legend, Gordie Howe, and his wonderful wife Colleen. I asked Gordie many questions about his successful career, but the greatest thing he said was, "It was always my dream to be an NHL hockey player. I never went out on the ice without giving it everything I had. I always expected to win, and when we lost, all I could think of [was] winning the next game."

One day in his late 60s, Gordie sat in a big chair in our living room and did what he loves to do, visit and tell stories. He had lunch in that chair and all together he was there for several hours. When he went to get up, I had to help him because the arthritis had stiffened him up during those hours.

He was scheduled to play in an oldtimers game that night at the Coliseum, and as I helped lift him up out of that chair, that wonderful giant of a man softly said to me over his pain, "Jim, not to worry, we're going to win the game tonight, and I'm going to score the winning goal!" He played well that night and they won. *Wow*. That's how we should all want to end up after we have fought and won the battles of life, stayed on course and made those dreams become a reality.

Keep the end in mind, not the potholes, not the pain, not the rejection along the way. Your dream is your compass and your honing device. It is your North Star.

Keep the end in mind, not the potholes, not the pain, not the rejection along the way. Your dream is your compass and your honing device. It is your North Star.

Our dream has been to be financially free and to encourage other people to get more out of life by reaching inside of themselves to find out what makes them tick, and then go for it. Freedom always comes with a price and a great deal of focus. Every Olympian says the same thing when interviewed about their achievement. It was always my dream to be here. Then they follow that up with the discipline, the regime, the eight-to-10 hours of training every day, fighting through the pain and—staying the course

I want to *challenge* you today to lock onto your dream and then stay the course until you get there. Keep going until you have completely fulfilled the mandate that you were brought here to fulfill.

I want to challenge you today to lock onto your dream and then stay the course until you get there. Keep going until you have completely fulfilled the mandate that you were brought here to fulfill.

Chapter 11: Victim Mentality—Are You a Victim?

If you're a self-declared victim, you can't get there from here. The road gets very steep when you have accepted that you are a victim. An incredible new life awaits you the minute you recant from victim mentality. Too bad it doesn't disappear that quickly.

I've seen guys with their limbs blown off who are running companies, running for political office and running marathons on prosthetics. I see ugly people doing beautiful things, and I see beautiful people doing ugly things. It's all in how they see themselves. I met someone last night with every disease imaginable, including Parkinson's. He's been on death row, medically speaking, several times in the past several years. He also walks several miles a day, is a successful financial services agent, and has earned two postgraduate degrees during these difficult days. Right now, he's writing an exam and another one in two weeks, between two operations. You could say he is a victim of circumstances, but he declared yesterday, as he spoke with great difficulty, that he definitely is not a victim and on his way to perfect health!

I just met a young couple in an East Coast city a few weeks ago. Both had been brought up in foster homes, one being an orphan and the other with parents who were incapable of raising their kids. She has a medical science degree and is very successful in her chosen line of work. The young man started working in coffee shops, and when I saw him just days ago, he was spending a few hours in his second successful shop of his own. He was in the throes of doing a third that will include a coffee roaster. His goal is to be "the" coffee place in the Maritimes.

These two could easily have decided that, as victims of a bad upbringing, they would settle for welfare and food stamps the rest of their lives. Millions do, and they complain bitterly about those who've stepped out and stepped up to help make the world a better place; people who hire employees, pay taxes at every level and donate to those in need, while personally giving of their time to Little League, coaching, and boys' and girls' clubs, and often volunteering at their houses of faith every week.

I know some entrepreneurs who pay over $200,000 a year in property taxes alone. These taxes pay for schools and streets, sewer and water lines, electric power grids, fire stations and many jobs for those who work to do all of this and oversee it. They could say forget it. They could say that because they feel that they're not appreciated and people actually are demonstrating on the streets about people like them, they'll just stop. They'll stop with the 15-hour days, sell everything they've got, give it to the poor and join them, thereby becoming part of the problem instead of part of the solution!

We live in a truly mysterious time in history. It is a time that may soon cause the world to retreat back into a medieval society unless we begin to shrug off our need for entitlement and victim mentality and begin to take responsibility for our own lives.

> We live in a truly mysterious time in history. It is a time that may soon cause the world to retreat back into a medieval society unless we begin to shrug off our need for entitlement and victim mentality and begin to take responsibility for our own lives.

I asked a friend the other day how he was doing, and he said, "My thumb is much less shrivelled than it's been!" I high-fived him. You can overcome victim mentality.

So what is victim mentality? Someone who:

- Is very self centered
- Believes someone else is creating, or has created, all the problems they have
- Sees the negative in every situation
- Can't see the forest for the trees
- Is fearful and worried about things that are never going to materialize
- Makes mountains out of molehills as a profession

Chapter 12: Have Absolutes Become Obsolete?

As a rule, destiny does not happen by accident.

Travelling with the right credentials is vital these days, and so it is with life itself. Don't expect to get through customs without a passport. I've heard many people say, "I would sure like to travel out of the country but I don't have a passport." Sorry, some things you just have to do if you want to get the desired results.

Absolutes can help you get there from here. In fact, it is difficult to get there from here without them.

> Absolutes can help you get there from here. In fact, it is difficult to get there from here without them.

Fundamental principles are being challenged every day, and some believe there are no such things as absolutes anymore.

Would you fly with a pilot who didn't have formal training and who didn't follow FAA protocol? Would you submit to having brain surgery from a doctor not formally trained or willing to follow standard medical procedures for the operation? I recently had cataracts removed and I'm glad standard procedures were followed. The result, voila! My eyesight is great. It still always has a lot to do with who has the instruments in their hands.

As absolutes continue to become obsolete, and speaking truth becomes old fashioned, our society has become deeply flawed and is quickly coming apart at the seams. When you don't stay on your side of the road in oncoming traffic, sooner or later you crash. That is an absolute; however, it becomes much more complex than that. People are on their way to a slow death almost every day for scorning almost every absolute that's ever been established. There are, in fact, many new absolutes as well. We now know if you smoke you'll likely get lung cancer at some point. The absolute was always there; we just hadn't discovered it yet.

None of us would fly with an untrained pilot who hadn't taken the necessary training or put in the hours needed to qualify for taking passengers with her. We wouldn't trust a pilot who didn't follow the absolute fundamentals of flying; nor would we go out into the ocean with someone who didn't know how to read charts and use the instruments and operating systems on the boat he or she was piloting. (I love the sea and have been a seaman on my own vessels on the West Coast of Canada and the U.S for 25 years.) Your safety and often your life depend on the fact that the operator learned, practised and experienced the fundamentals of handling the specific craft and the ways of the sea. My last boat had 100 systems and I knew them all. Not bad for a sanguine personality type.

There was a plane crash recently. All 50 or more passengers and crew were killed. It seems that icing was suggested as the initial cause but the pilots may have also left the plane on autopilot too long. The rule is that when icing occurs, the pilot takes the controls from the autopilot so they can feel the changes taking place early enough to avert disaster. Someone decided to ignore that rule just a bit too long.

In the same way, if your expenses are greater than your income, you will go bankrupt whether you are an individual, a business, an organization, or a city, state or country. It is a basic absolute that is ignored every day, especially by governments at all levels. You cannot trust in an entity that consistently runs a deficit, as it will crash and burn right before your eyes. Don't be one of those people, and don't vote for one who goes there, or advocates it either. They may be able to do everything else right, but if the finances are not there to sustain their promises, commitments and lofty ambitions, the system will eventually end up in total collapse. This is something we are seeing every day during these times, even though many wilfully turn a blind eye to these obvious challenges.

You can't fool around with absolutes, and yet many try to cheat the system, take shortcuts or rebel and ignore the fundamentals of life and living. In the long run, the results are painful and sometimes even brutally harsh for these individuals.

You might ask, "Are you recommending conformity at all costs?" Are you kidding? I have never been a conformist! There's so much room to be edgy, to project your personality into how you present yourself. There are a million ways to do things differently without breaking the fundamental rules of the road, which most likely will cause you to crash eventually. You can have an unconventional, fun-filled, crazy, wonderful life, if that's what you aspire to, and you can do so while still acting responsibly, living by the rules, and working from fundamentals that are vital to achieving one's destiny and keeping it intact.

> You can have an unconventional, fun-filled, crazy, wonderful life, if that's what you aspire to, and you can do so while still acting responsibly, living by the rules, and working from fundamentals that are vital to achieving ones destiny and keeping it intact.

I have often seen religious people suddenly discover that they can have a drink without violating the absolutes they once felt they needed to adhere to. So that's okay, but then I find them making a big deal about it, even flaunting the fact, and at times overdoing it, as in crossing the line of the absolutes they do believe in! Nada. They often go far beyond those who've never had any issue with the subject to begin with. It all seems so intriguing and innocent at first but it seldom ends there.

None of us want to be operated on by a surgeon who doesn't follow standard norms and procedures for an operation. When our life depends on it, we're in the box. Yet when it comes to violating the more philosophical and moral fundamentals that could also kill us, many would like to think absolutes no longer apply and we want out.

How can you have any confidence in that approach when your very soul may depend on it?

Why do we demand that basic fundamentals and absolutes be followed in one area and not in another?

We accept or demand procedures that give us desired results in some areas, but when methods, structures, belief systems or procedures cause us to change our behaviour or our lifestyle, we have a tendency to question and demean everything to do with that process or belief system.

Political correctness, which I've referred to earlier, and our fear of being clear about beliefs that may step on someone else's toes often cause us to wimp out on certain absolutes. The word hell can turn some people upside down if used in a religious context, and yet, those same people often use the word 20 times during a 30-minute speech or conversation. What is that? You say oranges and apples. I say, you decide.

We twist and turn in the most unusual ways to make things happen to justify our personal desires and ends. We'll pick at one or two things a politician says or does; and then call them down as being an evil two-headed monster, although we would think it most preposterous and unfair if we were judged by one or two of our least favourable traits. We would say, "You're not seeing who I really am. My core, fundamental beliefs are sound and well founded!"

Lest you think I'm condemning, I am not. Never throw the first stone or the fifth. One day near Christmas, I had a cult person come up my driveway to talk to me. He had been harassing my daughter at the door several times in our absence. His opening line was, "So what do you think of Jimmy Swaggart?" This was just after his fall from grace. I said, "But for the grace of God, there go I."

None of us are more than a heartbeat or two away from moral disaster. Thank God there is a way back. The prodigal son became the favourite when he repented his ways and came home. We all make mistakes but we can all come home and be restored. Redemption is an awesome thing.

> We all make mistakes but we can all come home and be restored. Redemption is an awesome thing.

Grace Is Amazing

The peripherals and the expression of how we live out our fundamental philosophies, or belief systems, can and will change. Everything around us changes all the time. If we can hold on to some fundamental absolutes, our lives can be so much less frustrating and much more peaceful and fruitful. When things change we must check out the trajectory or the direction of the change and where it is or could take us next, because, as we just said, change is inevitable but it often goes towards the lowest common denominator. Seldom does change build more character, discipline, clarity or righteous living. It usually moves away from a defined Deity to a humanistic paradigm of some kind. Check out how most universities were founded and what their prevailing message is today.

There are three fundamental principles regarding finances that begin to move people from living lives of economic chaos and quiet desperation to financial freedom. They are so basic that they're difficult to express without sounding overly simplistic.

Yet millions of seemingly very brilliant people never pass Economics 101.

The First Principle, Live within Your Means.

Don't spend more than you make. Your *income* must be greater than your *out* go. Don't go into debt. Pay-as-you-go. Credit kills. Many are physically dead and buried because they succumbed to insurmountable debt, which all began with one credit card purchase.

Number Two, Pay Yourself at Least 10 Percent out of Every Paycheque.

We pay the credit card company, the mortgage company but never ourselves: something we should do first. In other words, save it. Without this fundamental principle, economic hardship will definitely dominate our lives. Most agree in concept, but too few follow it. You actually write the cheque to your savings account every time a cheque comes in. Without this principle in place, when our income is interrupted for months at a time— and at some point it most likely will happen—we soon become very anxious about how we will survive, or at the very least maintain our lifestyle.

The Third Fundamental, Give 10 Percent to Someone Less Fortunate than You, or to an Organization That Does This.

I continue to be amazed at those who say they care so much but never reach into their own pockets to prove it. They are all about helping as long as "someone else" is doing the helping. I have news for those folks: "someone else" is already doing it, but we all must carry some of the load. When we do, we then also share in the blessing it gives. It is the best investment you can make. The returns are amazing. More later.

Following these three simple fundamental principles is the beginning of the miracle of becoming part of the solution instead of part of the problem. It means that you will become financially free. As we have witnessed in the recent financial meltdown, none of the above has been the rule during the past several decades, and that is why we find ourselves in chaos and remorse.

Few people can live even six months on their financial reserves, as we found out; even General Motors couldn't do it. This astounded me.

> Few people can live even six months on their financial reserves, as we found out; even General Motors couldn't do it.

The second principle is self-gratifying. It's easy to say, "Sure, I can understand how that can make the world, especially my world, better in the years to come." To the third one we might say, "Just a minute; how do I benefit from that one?"

First of all, who said anything about you benefitting? If it always has to be about you, you're hooped, and you ain't goin' anywhere soon! Significance is not in your future if your first question is, "What's in it for me?" The hidden, locked-up little secret is that there's so much in it for you when you learn to reach out to others unabashedly, that you can't even imagine how incredible it is. "The secret of real living is giving!" What you covet and hold onto, you lose, and what you give multiplies and blesses you over and over again. "You can get almost anything you want but it can bring leanness to your soul."

> The hidden, locked-up little secret is that there's so much in it for you when you learn to reach out to others, that you can't even imagine how incredible it is. "The secret of real living is giving!"

Know What You Believe

Until you know what you believe, you are like a leaf tossed in the wind or a wave in the sea, constantly picking up on the latest concept or idea and never knowing for sure if you've got it right or not.

Being open minded is good, but if you are not rooted and grounded in a belief system, there will always be turmoil, frustration and doubt about who you are and where you are ultimately going to end up. When the Winter Olympics took place a while ago in beautiful Vancouver and Whistler, BC, Canada, the lessons learned from these Olympic athletes were amazing.

Every medalist tells you that there came a time when they knew exactly what they were all about in their chosen endeavour. After that, their destiny was never in question, and every morning they knew exactly what they had to do, why they were doing it. They quit navel gazing or questioning how the judges judged or whether the Olympics Committee was a credible organization or even if the Olympics were relevant in today's world. Instead they got something done that changed their life and the lives of others forever. There is a time to quit questioning, grab some absolutes you can live with and get on with life.

Hang onto this, because at some point you have made or will make that kind of a decision. Somewhere in these pages there may be an hour or a flash of time that will bring clarity to what your destiny is. It will be your hour of decision! Millions have come to that point in their life where they knew that they knew that they knew what their destination station was going to be. What a thrill.

> Millions have come to that point in their life where they knew that they knew that they knew what their destination station was going to be. What a thrill.

It may be your time to say yes, I believe. You may end up saying yes to the biggest decision of your life to date even though at times it may come with the need for humility, sacrifice, scorn and derision. It comes with great rewards as well. We have had to make those decisions. Don't be afraid to think about these things from a spiritual perspective. You'll often find those whose destiny has been renowned feel that God had something to do with it.

The theme here for our Olympics was "I believe." Wow, I love it. It has been one of my lifelong themes. No concept, no ideology, no career, no man-made belief system is perfect, as we as humans define perfect. There is another perfect that we see when viewed from a certain distance, angle, or perspective. The earth from the moon looks pretty much perfect. Insects, birds, and other creatures of nature from a certain perspective look perfect. We look at a field of tulips or a hillside of turning leaves in the fall and we say, "Wow, beautiful." It really does seem perfect, and for those few moments, time stands still, and then we have to board the bus.

We look at the athlete on the stand or in the blocks, or the beautiful model in the Miss World Contest, and we say, "perfect"; but these individuals all got there because they made a decision and then worked at the idea or an ideal that was far from perfect in the beginning. Then they made it happen. So it is with our move to significance and fulfilment—our destiny.

These individuals all got there because they made a decision and then worked at the idea or an ideal that was far from perfect in the beginning. Then they made it happen. So it is with our move to significance and fulfilment—our destiny.

As I am writing this today, a friend of ours is on her way to China to represent Canada in the Miss World Contest. What she has had to do and endure in preparation for this event was excruciating. She has done it for a cause she's been championing for several years, that of eliminating human trafficking. This young woman in her early twenties has already presented her cause to world leaders and people who care from every walk of life. She has absolutes in her life; she has a purpose and a focus that drives her to do more every day, just like the Olympic athlete. We should all be so purpose-driven.

There are many things that I don't know or fully understand about my faith, but I know people whom I respect, who know and understand things that I don't understand yet. Most importantly, however, I know and I believe the basic fundamentals of my faith with enough certainty that I can, without hesitation, give an answer to it anywhere, any time. These fundamentals are good enough for me to get my running shoes on first thing in the morning and get going.

Your belief system should be your rock, your North Star, your guiding light and the screening process through which all of your decisions are made. Be sure that whatever or whomever you believe in is bigger than you are. It has to be something or someone that gives you authority to do what you do, and maybe even the power to do it. If your belief system does not light you up for a lifetime and give you hope and assurance for this life, and the one hereafter, you may want to find one that does.

> "Your belief system should be your rock, your North Star, your guiding light and the screening process through which all of your decisions are made.

Don't try to be Miss Universe, or the champion athlete right out of the chute. Do as they did, come to practice just as you are, submit to the rigours of the climb and you'll be on your way to getting there from here! I look at the numbers of people in the gyms and those running in the park. You don't have to be perfect, just a willing soul, ready to do what it takes and to serve others along the way.

Belief, and acting on your belief, makes you whole. It destroys the inferior, diminishing and lowering thoughts you may have about yourself and launches you into a whole new world. You were made in the image of God and He makes no junk. Trust Him, obey Him and you will succeed in finding purpose and meaning in life. Look it up. Psalm 1:4-5 (Okay, I'll stop with the preachy stuff).

> Belief, and acting on your belief, makes you whole. It destroys the inferior, diminishing and lowering thoughts you may have about yourself, and launches you into a whole new world.

Make sure you have an anchor that holds when the storm clouds come. That's another absolute. The storms will surely come, perhaps already have for many of you, but when you know who holds the future, you can move forward with confidence and faith in that future. Remember that problems are the normal state of life. Most of us wake up to a whole new batch of them every day. It never ends, but with the right attitude and a clear shot at the summit, the going is not that tough.

> The storms will surely come, perhaps already have for many of you, but when you know who holds the future, you can move forward with confidence and faith in that future.

I am absolutely sure that when you find your absolutes, life will be better than you could ever imagine. Not everyone will like you, but you'll have the power, strength, confidence and poise that give you the capacity to love unconditionally, and to reach out to your fellow man in ways you never dreamed possible. Don't allow a stubborn self-will to keep you from God's best for your life. Only when you know that you know, can you be accepting of others without malice, pride or discontent. Now you are working in harmony for a better future for you and yours.

> I am absolutely sure that when you find your absolutes, life will be better than you could ever imagine. Not everyone will like you, but you'll have the power, strength, confidence and poise that give you the capacity to love unconditionally, while reaching out to your fellow man in ways you never dreamed possible.

None of us are perfect and all of us have doubts and fears from time to time as we waffle on the absolutes we've chosen to put our faith and trust in. That's what makes us human and that's why we need redemption, grace and forgiveness. We spend our whole lives working towards those moments in time when we have our whole act together. May we all find peace, favour and blessing on the life journey we have chosen to take.

> May we all find peace, favour and blessing on the life journey we have chosen to take.

A Rendezvous with Destiny

Doing the Right Things

Doing the right things, even imperfectly, can bring you to a whole new and exciting place. Doing the wrong things, even if you do them to perfection, will never get you to your destiny.

Chapter 13: Get It Done for Pity's Sake

It's Relatively Easy to Start, Hard to Get It Done

People who "have it," who have traction on their journey to their destiny, get things done in a timely fashion.

More sales have been lost, more deals have gone awry, and more dreams have been shattered, because follow-through did not happen with consistent intensity right to the finish line! Many others never got traction or serious notice because they didn't do adequate discovery to find out the need, dream or desire of the potential client.

How many times have I said in a moment of emotion or genuine interest, "Sure, I'll do that for you." Instead, I should have taken inventory of my time, my skills, my support mechanism, my interest in the idea, and how deep the pool was before I dove in. The result was huge disappointments, major stress, loss of face and reputation—with whole communities at times.

We often end up delegating these ill-fated promises, but when we delegate, we must set dates and times to pursue the project until it is *finished*. Just like that program you download on your computer, unless you continue until you see the word "finished," all your efforts are in vain.

Doing it now and doing it well means walking through the details so that everyone understands their roles and responsibilities regarding the project, and then having them repeat it back to you verbally or in writing. In this way both of you know where you want to go with this. It is so much faster to do it right the first time than to do it over and over again.

If you're feeling my emotion here, you're feeling the right thing. Have you ever had people work on websites or other technical projects for you? If you have, you can identify with my pain—current techies excluded. We've been in that business for years and patience hasn't always been my virtue!

One of the biggest reasons why businesses fail and people end up broke is because they don't close the deal. Nothing happens until someone makes a sale, and a sale is not a sale until the money has been transferred from the bank of the buyer to the seller. I'm sure you know that everyone's income, including yours, depends on a sale being made somewhere in a free market economy. If it doesn't, the income came from borrowed money. Think about that for a minute.

> Nothing happens until someone makes a sale, and a sale is not a sale until the money has been transferred from the bank of the buyer to the seller.

If you are a clerk in a municipal or city hall, you will soon not have an income if someone out there is not making sales to create income to buy houses and other properties; all toward making a profit so they have the money to pay the taxes your income comes from.

It is difficult for some folks in the education field or sciences to understand that all of their income and research money comes indirectly from those of us who are getting our hands dirty twelve hours a day to keep the economy going, so that funds are available to pay for those jobs and disciplines. What is a little hurtful at times is that we are looked upon as a lesser species by some of those same folks.

We just found out what happens when cars and appliances don't sell any more, even when houses don't sell. Complete towns and sections of cities have disappeared; the schools, the labs, and the professors who often scorn the free market system—suddenly gone. So at least say thank you! How's that for a rant!

Procrastination is a big factor here. "Doing it now" is a great thing to get used to doing. The freedom that comes from doing it now: making the phone call now, going to see the client now, getting the paper work done now, paying your taxes monthly and submitting them on time, every time. The angst we place on ourselves by procrastinating actually leads to health problems that at times can be fatal. Stress is a killer. So doing it now is really not much of an option.

> "Doing it now" is a great thing to get used to doing.

Have we said enough? I ache for those who just constantly don't do the practical stuff that needs to be done in a timely fashion in order to keep their world barely functioning. Keep life simple. Don't take on too much and get the basic things *done*!

Do It Their Way Is Another Way to Get It Done More Efficiently

As someone said, "It's about your client, stupid."

Young people today are sometimes more guilty of this than older people, but we all slip into the ditch on this one from time to time.

Take painstaking efforts to explore your client's wants and needs before you make a presentation. This represents three quarters of the sale. Once you've discovered these—and only then—you can begin to match your product or service to your client's needs.

I have walked out of many an automobile showroom or real estate open house with money still burning a hole in my pocket because the sales person didn't get creative. He or she didn't offer suggestions of how a deal could be put together, or looked to see if there was another product or another way to structure a deal that would fit my needs, other than the obvious ones at hand. This concept applies to any presentation being made to convey an idea or philosophy to a person or group of people.

Find a Need and Fill It

The toughest thing for me to remember is to prepare and ask the right questions for roughly the first 10 minutes of a presentation. My son and I once lost a multi-million-dollar deal because we didn't pursue the right line of questioning. It was a costly lack of preparation. We could feel our chances slipping away right under our feet.

We had all kinds of people come to present website ideas to us in the early days of the online industry. Most were just their own pet ideas of how our site should look, feel and function, and all were given without once asking us what we needed and were looking for. These people were ushered out of the boardroom in a similar way that Donald Trump ushers out the loser every week on the television show *The Apprentice*.

Then it happened! A small firm came in and spent our entire first appointment asking us what we wanted and needed. Before they left, they gave us a ballpark price, which was much less than the previous big guys. Over the next seven years, they were paid handsomely for their pragmatic and client-centred approach.

The client's needs always come first! We *serve* the client. What a concept. That's how destiny is fulfilled.

The client's needs always come first! We serve the client. What a concept. That's how destiny is fulfilled.

Goals

Getting it done begs the question: getting what done?

For the rendezvous with destiny to be fulfilled many goals will need to be reached. Here is some sound advice on how to achieve them. They are often referred to as having goals that are smart.

Goals should be:

Specific - The more detailed and descriptive the more effective

Significant - The more they are a big part of your destiny the better

Stretching - They should be big enough to make you stretch

Measurable - They need to be measurable daily/weekly/monthly

Meaningful - They need to mean something to your total life

Motivational - They need to be exciting enough to inspire you

Agreed upon - Those involved in the process must agree

Attainable – A key factor is just beyond your reach but still possible

Acceptable - They must be acceptable within the system

Relevant - They must fit in with today's world

Reasonable - Don't be totally crazy or outrageous

Rewarding - It should be worth it in the end

Time-based - A goal is a dream with a deadline

Tangible - You should be able to describe it on an elevator ride

Teachable - People who are a part of it must understand it

Trackable - You should always know how you are progressing

Chapter 14: Unity

The ease and thrill of working or living in a unified environment is everybody's dream. The efficiency on a unified team is the ultimate, and the speed at which decisions are made is amazing. People volunteer even for the hard jobs on a team like this.

If destiny is to be achieved, in most cases, one has to learn how to work with people, how to work within a system or even—God forbid—within the rules, but most importantly, in a cooperative fashion. It's so much less frustrating than being an outsider all of the time. You can make new rules when you get there, if you still think it's necessary.

Unity

The degree of unity in an organization is the difference between strength and weakness, winning and losing, succeeding or failing. Teams, businesses, and organizations that are unified are the only ones that have a chance of making it through the rain intact, and it is bound to rain sooner or later. In fact, I think I feel some drops right now!

Who in the organization is responsible for it? Unity can only be experienced when the majority of a group is committed to it. It's not the responsibility of a few. It takes a commitment from everyone in the group because it must be a fundamental hallmark of an organization. We all need to be catalysts or agents for unity if we want to get there from here expeditiously

Who and what causes disunity, aside from ego and greed? Many things do. Here are few rather obvious, but recurring, unity busters.

Innuendos

The other day as I was leaving a function, I heard someone say to a buddy on the way out of the session, "So, what did you think of *that* speech?" Someone else at the same meeting said, "What do you think of *that* policy?" Those who speak in negative innuendos take three people down: themselves, the person they are talking to, and the person and or organization they are talking about. Absolute poison emanates from seemingly innocent innuendos, and then unity is destroyed. Always take your concerns to the source where they can be resolved or at least explained.

Self-Centred and Narcissistic Individuals

When a group has a few dominant self-centred, narcissistic individuals who put their own interests, ideas, and programs ahead of, or in opposition to, that of the majority of the group, things can become very difficult.

People with this bent have difficulty being part of a group of any kind and yet they like to have a crowd to pontificate with, complain to, and be recognized by. These people have to be confronted, especially when the harmony of the group is disrupted on a regular basis because of their activities.

Nitpickers

I went to an establishment the other day and asked for a specific clerk who was supposed to know something about what I was looking for. Someone there said, "Oh, he's not with us anymore.

We just couldn't afford to keep him because he was nitpicking us to death!" This activity can be very aggravating and destructive. The sign outside reads, "Help wanted. Nitpickers need not apply." These folks can find something wrong with absolutely everything that is said and done. They slow things down and drive everyone crazy.

> The sign outside reads, "Help wanted. Nitpickers need not apply." These folks can find something wrong with absolutely everything that is said and done.

Lack of Self-Esteem

Lack of self-esteem is the biggest reason why some people put other people down. Subliminally, they think it enhances their position with peers and superiors, when in the end it's very destructive and causes them much loss of credibility. Ironically, this is the very thing they are trying to gain.

They are so often wrong in their comments because their motives are wrong. Being "right" greatly strokes their self-esteem. In the meantime, untold disruption is caused and many reputations are destroyed simultaneously.

You have to fix 'em or root 'em out, or they will destroy your organization. The problem is, they are often very good producers, which makes it very difficult to remove them from the scene. Sometimes they can function within a system and be given a fair amount of autonomy within those parameters. Most of the time, we just live in hope on that one. I still think of this as a possible solution, although I know it seldom solves the problem, and sometimes makes it even worse.

Manipulative Discourse

Some people can only converse with you if they have an agenda. This is usually motivated by ego or greed, and sometimes by the same lack of confidence we just talked about. They are never solution oriented or creative; they are often casting aspersions on someone in leadership or putting "in question" policies, projects or methods of operation that the organization has endorsed or is seriously contemplating.

I am really a fun-loving guy with an insatiable bent towards creating positive attitudes, harmony and unity in organizations and other relationships. However, I believe that manipulative discourse is thoroughly and absolutely despicable. In the end, these people always want to look good and sometimes suggest that they be placed in the particular leadership position in question. The Bible even comments on them. God says, "Six things do I hate—no, seven: someone who causes discord among the brethren!"

Fringe People

These folks are always found doing hallway meetings (which we do not allow in the organizations where I'm involved). Fringe people yap around the edges, creating havoc with everyone they come in contact with. It's their way of getting recognition and attempting to achieve superiority. They are seldom producers, so the only way they can get noticed is to throw sand in the gears and watch the sparks fly.

> Fringe people yap around the edges, creating havoc with everyone they come in contact with.

Here are a few simple ideas and some profound principles on how to make unity a reality in an organization:

1. Individual team members should deal with issues from a solution-oriented position and talk only to those they have an issue with and/or those who can do something about it.
2. No hallway meetings.
3. One should always take the high road, and not entertain gossip.
4. The Golden Rule is still as golden as ever. We should always be asking ourselves, "Would I want someone doing this to me, or saying this about me, or casting unfounded accusations or aspersions about my character or actions?" If it were the other way around, we would want them to act only in a way that would be comfortable for us; we should do the same by them.
5. Do and teach only that which the majority does and teaches. The power of a unified approach in an organization is unparalleled. Introduce new ideas only at appropriate forums and with the appropriate people in attendance.
6. Edification is rare these days but it's a powerful tool in the hands of a team member. Always be building people up, and not on a "yes but" basis. Edification comes back to you in spades.
7. Always take the high road. Have you noticed that when sports figures or military personnel are interviewed, they never buy into negative questioning? They just stay positive. The glass-is-half-full philosophy is the right perspective. There are all kinds of committees and people in leadership who, if approached respectfully, will take up causes and concerns, and then deal with them appropriately.
8. Speak health, growth, prosperity and unlimited potential to the listener. This is uplifting and so unusual in our society that it always ignites good conversation and good networking opportunities.
9. Be a possibility thinker. All things are possible with

God. So team up with Him and go for it!

10. Love—the love chapter: I Corinthians 13. We spell it out here.

11. Practice forgiveness. Holding grudges is like having both feet on the breaks. Be quick to say I'm sorry. Holding hurts, and an unforgiving spirit hurts you a lot more than it bothers the "rotten culprit" who did those mean and nasty things to you.

12. Only in serving each other do we truly become free! Serving with a willing heart will make your organization blossom and flourish. It becomes a thing of beauty and a place that you want to belong to for a long time.

13. Never lose hope. Never lose your dream. Never lose faith. Never lose your genuine love for each other. This is not your average business or organizational talk, but then who wants to be average?

Transparency

Lack of transparency inevitably creates mistrust and, sooner or later, mistrust shakes the foundation of any organization. All sensitive decisions and information should at the very least be in the hands of all the principals of the organization. Financial and legal issues should not be held in the hands of one or two individuals in an organization, because when things go bump in the night, those who are holding the bag go overboard.

> Lack of transparency inevitably creates mistrust and, sooner or later, mistrust shakes the foundation of any organization.

You can tell I'm a boater. Over the 20-plus years we spent on the Pacific coast, there has been more than one occasion when things went bump in the night. Anchors got dislodged on windy nights, pumps became inoperative, hoses decided to break or remove themselves from the pipes they were attached to, rocks showed up in "inappropriate" places, and docking in gale-force winds made things very exciting. If you've done much ocean boating, then you've done it all. It's part of the grand experience. Would we do it again? Absolutely. What's the point? Everyone on an ocean-going yacht needs to be aware of what is going on and must be available to help at a moment's notice.

Part of transparency is letting those affected by decisions, or those who need to execute decisions, be in on the project as early as possible. For sure you need to do this before it's been cooked or hatched. It's the only way to create trust and unity, and to effectively bring new ideas or concepts or products into play.

Many new organizations and companies are working at developing radical ways to create effective teamwork of the kind that evolves into a unifying effect, like that produced at Apple, Microsoft, Cisco and hundreds of other success stories.

This may be pretty tough stuff to deal with at times, but vital to any attempt at longevity in a group of any kind. This may be an overly simplistic view of the subject. However, I was told by a "gentleman" in a big downtown office with a view—a man who has had three companies crash due to personnel issues, and who was working on his second divorce at the time—that more transparency would have saved them all, businesses and marriages alike.

Chapter 15: Seventy Attributes of Those Who Find Their Destiny

This chapter describes the necessary characteristics and principles if a rendezvous with destiny is to prevail. These characteristics and principles are typical of those who are much more likely to discover their highest calling, and then move on to expeditious fulfillment.

Always perfecting
Striving to do things better every time out.

Joy-filled
Success and money do not make you happy, but generally, happy, joy-filled people achieve more than those with a dour disposition.

Diplomatic
Some treat diplomacy as if it were an infectious disease. They have won.

Balanced
Stubborn, pride-filled, unbalanced people are always veering towards one ditch or the other.

Buy into the system
Fringe people are never in, never happy, always finding fault. Those who work for change inside the system have much more power, peace and influence.

Positive attitudes
Seeing the glass half full, always healing, edifying and uplifting.

Ambitious
Faith-filled, dynamic, humble, co-operative people who love to move mountains. They are strong in action, humble in spirit and driven by purpose.

Opportunistic
They always find an opportunity, even in a crisis. It is what achievers of destiny are made of.

Enthusiastic
Enthusiasm means "God within you." "At the base and birth of every successful venture you will find an enthusiast." —Winston Churchill

Servant leadership
Fulfillment and long-term success only happen when we serve those we wish to lead.

Time managers
They make every hour count. They master it; they are not slaves to it. Get rid of the time stealers in your life. You know what they are. They rob you of a great future.

Do what you do best
We often work so hard on our weaknesses that we fail at our strengths.

Visionary leadership
They paint and describe the picture. They inspire people to come with them, because those who define—wins.

Focused

Keeps moving in the direction of their goal. We always end up in the direction of our gaze, and in the way our feet are lined up. Just ask a golfer. It's different than you think.

There's always a way

They know that at the critical moment the King always has one more move. Ever played chess? Someone said, "Everything works out in the end." So if that is true, why are things not working out? Because it's not the end yet. Notice the capital on the word King. Get to know Him.

Possibility thinkers

All things are possible if you believe. That's a promise.

Intentional living

What do you intend to do with your life, your profession, your faith? Declare it, and move on it now! Act on those intentions and win big! I think it is called finding your destiny.

Eat right

...as opposed to eating wrong. Know the rules; if you don't, find out. They are in this book in chapter 17, in the "Physical" section.

Exercise

The computer chair and the couch are killers. MOVE!

3 Levels of Maturity

1. Please help me.
2. I can handle it.
3. Please let me help you.

Don't skip any steps. You'll trip.

4 Levels of Thinking

1. Tangible
2. Conceptual

   3. Creative
   4. Visionary and faith-filled.

Most stay at level one and two. Four is rare air. Huge successes live here. Not everyone can get there and it's okay, because there's a lot of living to do, and a lot who find their destiny in steps 1, 2 and 3 as well.

7 things people want
   1. To belong.
   2. To be appreciated and recognized.
   3. To have security, while learning to live with uncertainty.
   4. To have freedom, while respecting the rights and freedoms of others.
   5. To have enough cash flow to live stress free.
   6. To have a reasonably comfortable lifestyle or more.
   7. To be significant and be making a difference— Destiny.

Strong foundation
The way up is down. Take time to build a solid foundation. What goes up too quickly will usually come down just as fast.

Everyone's a leader
Father, mother, team captain, bus driver, pilot, foreman, older sibling—leaders have influence. People with destiny use it prodigiously.

EGO
"Edging God Out" (EGO) leaves you on empty. A person wrapped up in themselves makes a very small package. It's not about you.

Financial stability
This is a desire of most, but a network of friends and family is the desire of everyone. You can have both to the full.

Honour parents
Long life follows.

Rooted in faith
If not there, then where?

Practical
A book could be written. The trouble is, it's impractical, nobody would read it.

Passionate
Only the passionate end up on top. Ryan Walter, NHL hockey player, Olympian and president and CEO of a professional hockey team, has written a book, *Hungry!*. Love it.

Belief
You've either got it or you don't. Good thing is, you can get it. It's free and it's only a decision away.

5 steps to financial freedom
1. Cover the basics: roof over your head, food on the table, etc.
2. Save 10 percent.
3. Give 10 percent. Really? Read the rest of the book. It's in here.
4. Find an opportunity.
5. Plan for the rainy day. And invest. *Don't skip any steps*.

Authority
Where does it come from? You decide where yours comes from. It had better not come from you alone. Only dictators and cult leaders can make that work, and only for a while.

Trustworthiness
Comes from doing what is right—always, without compromise.

Courageous

Go where others won't go. Do what others won't do. Become who others won't become. Achieve what others won't achieve.

People skills

Think about others' needs, dreams and desires, and do what you can to help. The golden rule is still in big time!

Compassionate

True, long-term successes have empathy and compassion. Walking in another's shoes endears you to your followers more than any other factor.

Character

Built over time, refined in fire, honed in battle, tested in victory.

Work ethic

A vital but somewhat lost art. It would be a great class to offer in high school and college. Instead we teach workers' rights and get the pants beat off us in the marketplace by immigrants who work hard.

Awareness

Maximizing the hand you have been dealt. Do your best with it.

Hygiene

An assumed attribute. We all know what the optimum is. We should try to get close to it every day.

Planner

As leaders or independent agents or entrepreneurs, if you do not plan today what you are going to do tomorrow, you wake up in the morning unemployed or at best very ineffective.

Communicator

Three key roles of leadership: communicate, educate and inspire. The leadership stool won't stand without all three.

Listener
Effective listeners are the best communicators, the best closers, the best liked. Ask questions.

Networker
The world becomes your oyster. Do it always, everywhere, every day, online and in person. Database, Twitter following, and Facebook are in; that's how it all works today. Don't try to do it without using them.

Patience
More is won by this virtue than by pushing to the front, even though a little push is needed at times.

Vision
Where there is none, people perish. The best leaders are the best visionaries, for sure.

Believer
The highest level of thinking; if you believe, all things are possible. Faith is the substance that creates everything. It is substance. Think about it. It always comes first.

Innovative
Innovators find a way. When all is dark, foreboding, and seemingly impossible, they still press on.

Influential
We all are influential, it's just a matter of the kind of message we communicate with our influence.

Family-oriented
Priorities are proven by our actions, not our words.

Perseverance
You can't win if you don't stay in.

Team player

What a concept. Team players pass the ball purposely and generously, to let their teammates score the winning goal. It's about the team and the W(as in we), not the personal achievement. They are edifying, not narcissistic. It returns in spades, beyond what you could ask or think.

Coach

Equips, trains, helps and inspires those on the field to win.

Mentor

Shows the way. Encourages and walks with the mentee.

Cordial

There is no place for arrogant or disparaging behaviour, if you want to get there from here in today's world.

Example

Leadership and influence can best be executed by example.

Goals

Without them, there is no good reason to get up in the morning. Remove the goal nets and the game is over.

Honesty

Simple, honest people can be trusted. Dishonest ones can't.

Focus

Focused people are a hundred times more likely to succeed.

Reader

It is very difficult to lead unless you read.

Conviction

It is the fire that burns deep in the hearts of those with a mission.

Passionate
Passion is how those with conviction express it.

Thinker
It should be on your To Do list every day. Take time for it.

Risk taker
Better to have tried than to die with the music still locked inside.

Consistent
A powerful concept that in the end transcends the dramatic, but spice it up along the way if you can. People listen more intently to those who do.

Teachable
Those who know it all, know very little.

Respectful
Respect and edification build amazing strength, and contribute to providing a powerful, seamless infrastructure where all participate.

Predictable
When a majority of the above attributes are in play, a positive, predictable result ensues. Almost everything you do will prosper.

When you have the right seed, the right soil, the right moisture, the right cultivation, and the right sunlight, you are pretty much assured of a bumper crop. Do the right stuff and you will have a rendezvous with destiny!

Chapter 16: The Discipline of Destiny

Don't you hate this part? This, however, is a big and vital part of seeing one's dreams come to fruition.

Let's see if we can get our heads around this one. If our dream is focused enough, our purpose is sure enough and our goal is intense enough, the discipline part will flow out of that. Destiny comes from the gut and drives us to the goal line.

One beautiful spring day is southern California I was watching a craftsman chiselling away at a huge block of granite. When he took a break I said to him, "What is this going to be when you are finished?" To which replied proudly, "A horse." I then asked how he'd get the block of granite to look like a horse, and he quickly said, "You just chip away everything that doesn't look like a horse." He wasn't doing this casually. He was enthusiastic and animated. His large lock of shiny black hair bobbed from side to side as he vigorously attacked the granite with his hammer and chisel. I said, "How long till you're finished?" He replied, "The plan calls for nine months."

Amazing how many things can take shape or give birth in nine months!

The man told me that he wasn't doing this by sight alone. He had drawings and measurements, stages and tools for each phase. He was there at 7:30 every morning without fail; sometimes seven days a week. Clean-up time began at 4:30 or 5:00, and took about an hour.

He stood back and analyzed his work every hour or so, and did measurements and settings to see if perfection was being achieved. He had others, some of them professionals, come and check his work almost every other day. He had a mentor who came occasionally to give suggestions and critique what was transpiring.

Granite is expensive and allows very little room for error. Fixing up mistakes is not a pleasant exercise here. When your work is out there for all to see, possibly for one hundred years or more, you want it to be perfect.

> When your work is out there for all to see, possibly for one hundred years or more, you want it to be perfect.

You might say, I saw someone just do this by sight. Yes, I have too. They are two different products. One is a science; another is a talent and a gift. They both start at 7:30 and they both take about nine months. One is perfect, the other is great art. I play the piano by ear and it's fun and entertaining, but they never ask me to play with the symphony.

The general in the army, the supersonic jet fighter pilot, the maestro of the orchestra and the tenor soloist, the astronaut, the athlete on the stand, the football, basketball, soccer, and hockey champion: All of these people got to be what they are by stringent, focused discipline, getting rid of all habits and weaknesses that don't look like those of a champion. They practice hours every day for over 20 years at times. They knew what their destiny was and they followed it, no matter how near, no matter how far, just as the lyrics of the song "To Dream the Impossible Dream" spells it out so beautifully.

So where does the discipline come from? Easy; it comes from knowing what you've been called to do, knowing your destiny, knowing and desiring with all that is within you to strive to the highest mark of excellence.

We recently received a Mark of Distinction Award from the DSA (Direct Sellers Association), a nationally distinguished organization, at a gala award banquet in Toronto, Canada. After speeches from the members of Parliament and the mayor of the city we were in (who incidentally at 93 was still holding office with full duties, still fulfilling her destiny), and after several of the Queen's Jubilee Medals were presented, it was our turn to receive the top honour of the evening. Later, I asked, why us? The gentleman in charge said, you had a destiny and you fulfilled it! That hit close to home, as we were in the final throes of getting this manuscript to the editors. People used to ask us why we climbed so high in our industry and my simple answer was because it was there. Mountain climbers do that, but not all of us are mountain climbers. I'm not. The key is to climb the mountain of your destiny.

> People used to ask us why we climbed so high in our industry and my simple answer was because it was there.

We have had several close encounters with Olympic winners, and we saw what it took for them to get onto that viewing stand, receive their medals and have the national anthem sung for them and their country. It is truly amazing and sometimes excruciating.

Last night we attended a sold-out concert in Palm Desert to hear Daniel Rodrigues, a first responder in the NYPD when the disastrous 9/11 happenings took place in New York. He is also an amazing tenor soloist who burst onto the scene during and after those events.

He told his story last night. He was born in Cuba and was a Cuban refugee who worked as a postman for several years before being accepted into the New York Police Department. He sang at Carnegie Hall when he was 17 but not again until he was 42! He knew that someday his musical talent would be recognized, but in the meantime he just sang in churches and at community events. He never stopped practicing and never lost his dream. Little did he know that it would take a major disaster to launch him out of his NYPD uniform and onto the world stage. He had a destiny. It was fulfilled.

We could tell one hundred thousand stories of those who have fought the good fight and won. It is tough to be a winner, tough to keep your head up when nothing seems to be happening, when nothing works. That's when you say to yourself "Tough Times Never Last but Tough People Do." —Dr. R.A. Schuller

> It is tough to be a winner, tough to keep your head up when nothing seems to be happening, when nothing works.

Thousands of people now train for marathons. It takes months of daily, painstaking effort to end up in the top 250 of a large marathon. People do that for a mere ribbon, but often won't do what it takes to win in the destiny they have been called to. I think we have made the point—just another piece of the puzzle.

Chapter 17: What Do You Have in Your Hands?

What we do every day determines our future. Almost everything that happens to you is in your hands. Your future is very much determined by your thinking, your choices and your decisions. Many people think and act as if their future is determined by luck or by their circumstances.

Opportunity abounds today and our chief aim should be to take advantage of those opportunities.

The only limits we have are those we place on ourselves.

> "If we did all the things we were capable of doing, we would literally astonish ourselves."
> Thomas Edison

> "How big would you dream if you knew you couldn't fail?"
> R.A. Schuller

To a large extent, we create our own future.

> "The very best way to determine the future is to create it."
> Peter Drucker

Success Is Predictable

"It is our duty as men and women to proceed, as though the limits of our abilities do not exist."
Pierre Teilhard de Chardin

We must learn from the experts.

"If you do what successful people do, nothing can stop you from eventually getting the same results they do. If you don't do what they do, nothing and no one can help you."
Brian Tracy

Luck is not a factor. Have you ever wondered how those who come to our country from all over the world with no friends, no network, no language skills, no money and no apparent opportunities become hugely successful? Luck? I don't think so.

So What Does It Really Boil Down to?

It boils down to knowing what you really want and having the desire and the commitment to follow through until you've achieved it. You don't need to know how, as much as you need to know specifically what your goal and your dream is. You *will* find a way.

Where will you be next year at this time? Will you be sitting there kicking yourself for not having moved up, or will you have at least a few people at your side who are excited to be there and to be moving along to achieving their goals and dreams.

For many of you, the time clock is running out. It is now or never. You will either begin to move out of the station today or you will forever live in regret that you didn't take full advantage of the opportunities in front of you.

The key to making this happen is to always keep that goal and that dream in front of you. This is not about killing yourself night after night, it is about confidently and excitedly moving forward every day by tangibly having done goal-oriented activities that will get you to your promised land.

Just point yourself in the direction of the future you want for yourself and

- Start moving in that direction.
- Keep moving in that direction.
- Never quit moving in that direction.

The story is told of two young men who frequently went to visit an elderly sage up in the mountains behind their town in the Alps. The wise old man always knew what they were up to. One day they went to see if they could trick him. They brought a dove with them and held it behind them, saying to the man, "We have a dove in our hands. Is it dead or is it alive?" If he said it was alive they would make it otherwise before they presented it. He quickly and wisely said, "Young man, it is in your hands."

Maybe the wise old man is speaking to you right now. Some of you may still be waiting and wondering when destiny is coming your way. It may be time for you to say, "I understand that it is in my hands." I will take up my bed and start walking. Walking by faith to I know not where, but knowing if I walk I will be guided to that purpose and plan that has been predestined for me.

"Put your hand in the hand of God and go out into the darkness and it will be better for you than a light and better than a known way."
The King's Speech

Chapter 18: I Didn't Sign Up for This

A famous movie star was asked what it felt like to have all this fame and fortune. What is it like? Well it's about days, weeks, and sometimes months of agony and torture, dotted with fleeting moments of adulation, recognition and feel-good times between gigs.

So why do you do it? It is my calling. It's what I do, who I am; it is my destiny.

Most movie stars say, sure I get up at 3:30 every morning. The limo or other vehicle picks me up at 5:00 a.m. and we work non-stop till 7:00 p.m. I get home at 8:00 and to bed at 9:00. Sometimes for 10 months straight this happens. Of course there comes a time years later when this all changes and the great life kicks in.

I answer that question by saying, "If you are willing to do what I do, you can live like I live." Not much mystery in that. The trite saying, "The harder I work, the luckier I get" still holds true.

> If you are willing to do what I do, you can live like I live. Not much mystery in that.

In most ventures, there's pain and drudgery and, at times, hours of boredom sprinkled in. The pilot who finally end up in the left seat of the 747 now finds himself in the air for 18 hours straight. How fun. Ugh. But he works for two weeks and has two weeks off. Somewhere before that time, there's been 10,000 hours of focus just to get to square one.

Then there's the nurse who finally gets the uniform and finds herself in operating room. On her first day she finds herself assisting in a life-and-death eight-hour emergency operation. The smile that greets her from the patient at the beginning of her next shift makes it all worthwhile. We could be here all day and never begin to scratch the surface on this topic, but the trite statement "there is no gain without pain" still holds pretty firm.

The secret is to have a calling that overrides all of the pain for the gain or sense of well-being at the end of the shift or of the extremely difficult labour negotiation session that lasts for three days and two all-nighters.

That's what happens when destiny calls. So what about all the summers with the kids and all that?

Eight to 10 months with some 15-hour days and some seven-day weeks, with the right vehicle, will begin to give you the lifestyle you desire. People of destiny all do that. The 10,000-plus hours came first. There are no shortcuts. Everything is not what it seems to be.

Before the glory is some gore-y.

Destiny people are engaged to some degree all the time. It's not their job, it's their calling. It is what they have chosen to do, even if it's just a vehicle to help them do what they are most passionate about during the eight hours after the eight-hour shift. One feeds the other. If you are still looking for ways to not be engaged or to avoid the price tag, your destiny has not found you yet. The rendezvous is still up ahead.

> "Destiny people are engaged to some degree all the time. It's not their job, it's their calling.

Today there are ways to shortcut some of this but the focus, the discipline, and the sacrifice still have to be there. I say 24 to 36 months of very intense effort are what young people today need to get their heads around getting it done. Intense focus is needed for "it" to get done in that time frame, but not necessarily more effort.

The glitz, the glamour, the recognition and the rewards come after the work is done. Steel is no good until it has gone through white heat. Not to worry, though, because when that steel becomes that beautiful vehicle, sculpture or glistening architectural marvel, all the challenges are forgotten.

There has to be a price if there is going to be a prize. You didn't sign up for this? Oh yes you did! Suck it up and get on with it!

Chapter 19: You May Already Have What You Are Looking For

Many folks who are looking for fulfillment may well be sitting on it.

Along the way they concluded that everything from their upbringing is no longer relevant. They think that the faith they once espoused is old fashioned, and unless they can tweak it almost beyond recognition to make it politically correct enough to fit into their lifestyle and the social norms of their peers, they may abandon it altogether.

I heard a testimony this morning from a relatively successful but very restless and unfulfilled gentleman who was invited by a friend to come to a mission with him one Saturday night because he was speaking there. That night, sitting amongst drug addicts, alcoholics and the most destitute of the city, he heard his friend tell these folks it was not too late for them to find healing, peace, redemption and fulfillment.

It was the message he had grown up with, and there in that place with folks much less fortunate than himself, he was suddenly jolted back to his roots and his childhood beliefs. Immediately the sky was bluer, the flowers more brilliant, the sun shone brighter and all that he had been looking for was there in a moment of time. It had been readily available to him all the time, but over the years he had slowly built a wall between himself and his roots, thinking he had to be more with it, or that new revelations were more relevant than those he'd grown up with.

Joy filled, he started several new successful ventures and foundations to help the underprivileged. Last Saturday night he celebrated his tenth anniversary of that night of enlightenment. You guessed it—he was the guest speaker at the mission! His call to destiny was complete. He was once again overwhelmed with emotion as he now shared his story of healing, redemption and fulfillment.

In Russell H. Conwell's book *Acres of Diamonds*, the story is told of the gentleman who spent a fortune and much of his life combing the world in search of diamonds, only to come home and find them on his own property.

Some people won't rest until they have explored all options. It's important for each generation to put their belief systems to the test, because if they don't really own them for themselves, they are of no value. The trite old saying, "Don't throw the baby out with the bath water," is an important one to factor in here.

So the point here is that we should always take inventory of the talents, abilities, contacts, connections, and opportunities that we already have. Even a second look at the principles and beliefs of our childhood may just have some relevancy at this point in our lives, sometimes long after our forays into other arenas may have proven not to work out that well.

Never let pride or stubborn self-will get in the way of doing something you can really be proud of.

Never let pride or stubborn self-will get in the way of doing something you can really be proud of.

It's always wise to look at the end game. When all is said and done, will all that has been said and done have been worth the trouble? Is it taking you to your promised land? Start with what you want said about you on your tombstone. What will your kids and those that know you best say about you when you have run your course?

> Start with what you want said about you on your tombstone. What will your kids and those that know you best say about you when you have run your course?

What will the last 10 years of your life be like? You are headed to those 10 years right now. The trajectory is in place. Yes, corrections can be made en route, but unless we jolt ourselves into a reality that has us going where we want to end up, we are now headed to that place.

Check out the folks who are there now, see what it is like for them. Pick your spot and then make the necessary adjustments.

Destiny Is Calling. What Will It Look Like for You?

Don't be discouraged or fretful about this scenario. There is always a way to make it better. The journey itself can be most pleasurable, so just get started now even if you are in or near that place. You can still make a huge difference in people's lives if you just sign up to serve. The opportunities are endless and the rewards very gratifying.

I meet ever so many retirees these days driving limousines, volunteering for a few hours a day or a week, counselling and consulting. Others are playing golf, taking flying lessons, getting degrees, becoming techno whizzes, and then teaching others their new-found skills. Some find ways to travel their wheels off to complete that bucket list in style! Many of these folks thought their useful days were over and their destiny complete before they found new meaning in service to their fellow sojourners for 20 or more years.

No matter where you are on the Richter scale, destiny is calling; someone is waiting for you to answer the call. You will have a joy-filled life if you do.

> No matter where you are on the Richter scale, destiny is calling; someone is waiting for you to answer the call. You will have a joy-filled life if you do.

Chapter 20: Entrepreneurism and Education—Two Options to Make Destiny a Reality

Entrepreneurism

Many find destiny in new entrepreneurial endeavours these days.

With the advent of the Internet, direct distribution has become more mainstream. Online shopping is exploding. Credible network marketing companies are becoming multi-billion-dollar entities, and dozens of new franchise opportunities have completely transformed the entrepreneurial world to meet today's norms and ideals.

These types of businesses are not for the faint of heart; however, for those who have what it takes, substantial rewards are available. I personally know folks who make millions every year in these entities. Each has had a positive influence on the lives of thousands of people for many years.

Those who've turned their distribution efforts into an online entity have developed a level of sophistication that has opened the industry up to a much broader segment of the population, from homemakers to high-level professionals.

If you choose to become an independent business owner who is affiliated with one of these companies, it is wise to find one with an in-depth training program driven by successful field representatives in close co-ordination with the mother ship. If the organization has an advisory group that works in partnership with the corporation, you have a much more secure entity.

Mentorship is vital in order to achieve success. It must have a program that includes continuing education, consistent and effective communication, and an inspirational component that keeps the troops on top of their game.

Recognition for outstanding achievement, along with major incentive programs, is a key factor in making it all come together.

You've probably guessed by now that we've had a long and successful career doing the above.

Looking at these entities from the outside, we can be intrigued and inspired. Hearing the success stories from those who've climbed to the summit may cause us to get tempted to engage. It's exciting, and it is worth it, but only those willing to pay the price will receive the prize.

Here are some tips we've learned along the way about growing fast and getting closer to reaching your destiny.

Build Your Own Team

You probably will need to build your own team. Listen carefully to the instructions of someone more experienced in the organization, someone who has mastered the art of doing what you are setting out to do. Building an organization from scratch is an onerous task. It takes a unique skill set, but if mastered it is one of most thrilling and rewarding things you can do.

Attend live training events and online webinars; acquire CDs, DVDs or downloads if available, and listen to them as many times as it takes until you've got it. If they don't have training materials of this nature, think twice about engaging.

Keep Your Mentor at Your Side

Keep your mentor at your side as long as possible, with debriefings after presentations. Have them do several for you. Before you venture out there with your own "wisdom" and "knowledge," do the following:

- Attend all the live or online sessions they hold, because in the early stages they will attract folks better than you can attract them yourself.
- Use their talents, their expertise, as well as their tools. It is called time, knowledge, experience, and skill leveraging. Don't try to be a pioneer in a well-established industry.

SW, SW, SW

Your biggest revelation at first is that some of your hottest prospective candidates don't get it. They actually say no! Get over this one quickly. SW, SW, SW stands for: some will, some won't, so what. You have to develop a fairly thick skin to get there from here in this discipline. It's a numbers game. Here's a great example to illustrate the point.

I was speaking to a very successful friend in the insurance business some time ago and I asked him what his specific job was as a manager in his industry. He explained, "I give birth and I nurture the babies."

Every January, he starts with 1,200 names derived from advertising, referrals and job inquiries. He then quickly whittles that list down to about 500 with a qualifying exam. From that list, he interviews the top 100 (the others are spares). Ten are placed in the system for training and active duty. Of the five who survive that exercise, one "keeper" comes out of that group for the long term.

My friend has done this for 25 years. He now has 25 very successful financial services executives who make seven-figure incomes per year (and so does he.) That's the way it's worked for me, and the many folks I know in the people business.

By the way, there are 50 other financial services execs making a decent living out of that office as well. Many are trainers and have other roles in the operation. The spinoffs of accountants, actuaries, lawyers and support staff are huge. It all started with one person with a will to win. He started the office with himself and a part-time assistant.

Patience and Overcoming Discouragement

If you have the intestinal fortitude to take on this type of leadership role, there are two major character traits that need to be prominent: patience, and the ability to overcome discouragement. You need a lot of both. Leading new inductees is like herding cats, something that seems almost impossible at times. On any given day you go home thinking that none of them have what it takes, when no production comes from any of them that day, or the previous several days! Hang in there. The cream will rise to the top. This is when you hit the hot tub, or gym, or even a good movie, just to brush off the waves of discouragement enveloping you and even causing you to doubt the industry or the specific company you are affiliated with. Start singing the "Tomorrow" song that the Disney people put into all of our hearts and minds.

> Leading new inductees is like herding cats, something that seems almost impossible at times.

Now it's time to remember the number of times this has occurred just before you had a huge burst of production which started a winning streak that lasted for months. Discouragement is a trait you cannot afford to entertain if you are going to lead successfully, long term. Remember, courage is in the middle of the word discouragement. So always remind yourself that you are a person of courage and patience when the troops are not performing as they should on any given day, or month.

> Remember, courage is in the middle of the word discouragement.

Nurturing

Nurturing is not a virtue that most of us men have in abundance; you need nurturing to get this baby off the ground. Those who do this best have daily contact with their new registrants for at least the first 14 days. Every other day should be spent with them, either on the phone or in person. On other days contact can be maintained electronically.

Skype is great. Your job is to help them participate in bringing folks into the program at least once in the first month, along with making those first important sales, if the program allows them to do so. They will all want to quit at least once during those first 14 days, which makes it so important to be in touch that day for resuscitation. This is a normal process and you'll learn to do it with the greatest of ease without worry or angst. It is normal.

Build Leadership

Here's a biggie. The thing that keeps so many from achieving ultimate success in the area of entrepreneurial leadership is the wounding of your ego when you bring on your first big winner who is better than you. Oh boy, can this ever set you on your heels. Pride is such a killer. Most of us can't bear to see an "underling" pass us in production, in popularity or in overall ability to perform.

I have news for you. If you don't get this taken care of, your future is limited. Sometimes you even have to reverse roles when this happens and, from time to time, allow them to mentor you and the rest of your group. Tough one, especially if they have a big ego as well. Open discussion is a must if success is to be achieved. Trust and transparency have to rule the day.

> Open discussion is a must if success is to be achieved. Trust and transparency have to rule the day.

If your company or system pays you for working in depth, drive it from day one. If longevity is to be achieved, build as deeply and as quickly as you can. Build relationships in depth. This inspires those who are in between to stay engaged and ahead of the game. It's also your security long term. This I would say is sage advice!

Become a Student of the Business

A small part of what it takes to turn it into a serious long-term proposition, one that becomes generational in nature if you stay with it, is to become thoroughly and proficiently skilled at the mechanics of a business of this kind.

Growth and Financial Stability

Make sure the company you affiliate with has a long history of growth and financial stability. Those are the roots that will hold it in place for your future.

Talk and Meet Face to Face

Don't let the Internet be your only source of reference. Talk to people in the business and contact the company yourself to find out exactly where they are at. Visit the company headquarters and get a tour, to check out the integrity of the company's claims.

Okay, that's it. These points are extremely important for growing faster than most in any industry. They must not be overlooked while in search of your destiny.

Education

Education is fundamental to the process. But it can also be a great hindrance if one doesn't go to the great halls of learning with strong beliefs and a singleness of purpose. *Many* lose their way, as many "isms" and other extreme philosophies are expressed as absolute truths, often by well-meaning professors. Such ideas can take young people down paths they never recover from.

We are in desperate need of good teachers, doctors, dentists, psychologists, engineers, pilots, musicians, nurses and other professionals. Many times, honing these specific skills is one's destiny. From a purely monetary perspective, an education is often a cornerstone to financial well-being.

I didn't know at all what I wanted to do with my life until my wonderful Dad nudged me into teaching. I am so grateful to him.

His nudge opened up new vistas and areas of understanding for me. Coming out from under a shelter and moving into the big tent was shocking for sure. I was confronted with very different ideologies and moral standards than I had growing up. It was a test of my beliefs, but also an opportunity to see life and the world from new perspectives. All of this was vital to everything that followed in my life as I mixed with thousands of people from all walks of life, eventually becoming their leader and mentor.

What happens at university is so much more than an accumulation of knowledge. It's about meeting professors and students of all backgrounds, the discipline of study, the involvement in sports and other group activities—learning to lead, to follow and to be a team player.

Forming focus and purpose and overall direction for one's life is a process not always accomplished if one just dives into the workforce at 18 years of age. You need to make time to contemplate options and get advice from those who give counsel as a profession. Most of the people you interact with on your journey to destiny have an education. If you don't have one, there will be a deficit in many of your areas of understanding and effective communication. Can you make it without a formal postgraduate education or profession? Yes. Bill Gates and thousands of others have proved it can happen big time.

If one does not have a natural bent or predisposition to a particular sport or entrepreneurial focus that you firmly believe is going to work for you, then get an education in a desired discipline. An education makes your life full, and your destiny will come to fruition.

> An education makes your life full, and your destiny will come to fruition.

I am a big proponent of education, especially as it relates to specific disciplines that you can make a good living at and contribute to the betterment of your fellow man. Education for the sake of education is okay but you may fall short in finding fulfillment in the long run.

Want Positive Economic Changes to Happen for You?

According to Robert Kiyosaki, you can engage in a great vehicle for financial success right here, right now.

Listen to what he says:

"If you want to go from the E/S (Employee / Self-Employed) Quadrants to the B Quadrant (where you build a substantial semi-absentee business as an Independent Business Owner), become successful by building a B Quadrant Business. It is one of the toughest challenges a person can take on, *but it is also one of the most rewarding*. Financial Freedom waits for you there if you are willing to climb the mountain." You can do this in real estate, in the franchise business and in a network marketing business and in many other businesses that lend themselves to duplication.

Kiyosaki continues, "These industries will teach you the skills necessary to be a successful B Quadrant Business Owner.

"The reason there are so many more people in the E and S Quadrants is because those are far less demanding than the B Quadrant, but as many of you well know, far less rewarding. E&S are all about you. B is all about helping others succeed, which always brings the greatest reward. Those wrapped up in themselves make a very small package."

Those wrapped up in themselves make a very small package.

If it were easy everyone would do it.

Kiyosaki goes on to say, "I had to overcome self-doubt, shyness and fear of rejection. I had to learn how to pick myself up and keep going after I failed.

"Another important trait I had to adopt was LEARNING TO BE A LEADER. This happens when you overcome your fears and can teach others to overcome theirs."

What a powerful commendation and accurate synopsis of a B Quadrant business. Go for it! Financial freedom can be yours.

The I Quadrant is the investment quadrant. This one is extremely vulnerable and takes as much education as any other discipline in the financial world. You will soon discover that.

BE CAREFUL but don't stay home.

A Rendezvous with Destiny

Wisdom and Destiny

Wisdom and destiny are intrinsically linked. The book of Proverbs is an amazing book, used as the centrepiece for many religions. It is also referred to by many who just seek wisdom because it was written by Solomon—a man purported to be one of the wisest who ever lived.

Listen to this as it pertains to wisdom that leads to destiny. Proverbs 3:16,17

Wisdom gives:
- A long life
- Riches
- Honour
- Pleasure
- Peace

"Wisdom is the tree of life to those who eat her fruit; happy is the one who keeps on eating it." (That list is pretty all-encompassing: it is the prerequisite that's tough to come to grips with at times!)

"Have two goals: wisdom that is knowing and doing right, and wisdom that is having common sense. Don't let them slip away because they fill you with living energy and are a feather in your cap. They keep you safe from defeat and disaster, and prevent you from falling off the trail." (3:21)

"With them on guard you can sleep without fear. You need not be afraid of disaster or of plots of wicked men for the Lord is with you. He protects you."

"If you exalt wisdom, she will exalt you. Hold her fast and she will lead you to great honour; she will place a beautiful crown on your head…and you will have a long life…a life of doing right is the wisest life there is… Carry out my instructions and you will experience real living!"(8:15)

Chapter 21: Pessimism versus Optimism

I was part of a very prestigious board some years ago. One day we found ourselves struggling with a seemingly difficult issue for several hours. The famous Dr. Clement Stone, founder and chairman of Combined Insurance Company of America, who was one of the board members, said, "I can't believe that this group of positive, dynamic leaders has taken this rather insignificant issue and turned it into a huge problem. It's solutions we need, it's solutions we need!" he bellowed, as he pounded his rather large fist on the board room table. Within five minutes the problem was completely solved.

Dr. Stone also wrote the book *The Success System That Never Fails.*

Optimists like Dr. Stone believe there's always a way until every possible solution has been exhausted. They never stop looking for a way to make things work. On the other hand, I've seldom seen a pessimist find their destiny satisfactorily. They always seem unfulfilled and unhappy. The pessimist always finds reasons why something won't work. They are seldom if ever happy with the results of their efforts or that of others. Pessimists take a most insignificant thing and turn it into a mountain in seconds, and then hold onto that negative perspective forever! I call them chronic pessimists or perpetual down-chunkers.

Pessimists sometimes focus more on illness instead of wellness. They often don't finish the verse, the chapter or the book. To be fair, overly optimistic people occasionally do the same from the other side of the coin. I choose heads.

Pessimistic people love to commiserate with a man named Job. They can spend hours talking about his troubles and how he suffered, without ever mentioning the enormous blessings of the last chapter of his life. They also skip the fact that Job said, "The very thing I feared the most came upon me." Be careful what you fear. If you don't know who Job was then look him up!

It's also tough to get there from here with a pessimistic approach to life. It's hard to move ahead when you have it in reverse all the time. The beeping sound alone can drive you nuts! Try the headlights for a change.

When the Going Gets Tough

We are all affected by traumas, yet it is so important to stay optimistic and to have empathy and compassion for those who can't see a way through. It is also incumbent upon us to help them find some hope while trying to find every possible solution to very difficult and, sometimes, overwhelming challenges.

Even powerful optimists can slide into being pessimists on any given day. I've sure done that many times myself and had to be jacked up by those close to me in order to get right-sided again. It's chronic pessimism that keeps you from accomplishing what you've been ultimately called to do.

Where would we be if Dr. Jonas Salk had been pessimistic about finding a cure for polio and Dr. Frederick Banting a solution for Type 1 Diabetes? Their willingness to pursue an optimistic outcome saved millions of lives. A fatalistic, pessimistic view would have caused millions to die.

You may say, "Haven't you been a bit rough on pessimists here? I thought we were looking for solutions to finding our destiny and getting there from here. Sometimes the medicine doesn't taste that good."

What we speak, we magnify, and what we magnify dominates, and what dominates our thinking, rules the day. Just remember, there's always a way!

What we speak, we magnify, and what we magnify dominates, and what dominates our thinking, rules the day.

Chapter 22: Without a System, Is Failure Inevitable? You Decide!

Many destinies are discovered and lost because their creators did not have a system to give structure and support to the discovery. Few lofty ideas ever come to fruition without one.

Systems

Take careful note. This is extremely important! It is vital information for those wishing to fulfill their destiny. We will keep it succinct.

For 18 years we lived quite close to a 7/11 store. That was 30 years ago. The store is still there, and the milk, bread and newspapers are still in exactly the same place. I can walk right to them blindfolded. It was all refurbished a few times but the owners kept the location of the "staples of life" in the same places. Each of the two owners was very successful.

There was a competing store in an ideal location on a corner in the other direction from our place. It was an independent amenities store. It carried mostly the same things that the 7/11 store carried but it went belly up at least six times in 15 years, until it was replaced by a restaurant that finally took over the prime location.

Why did the second store fail? They were great people with creative ideas: entrance west, entrance south, shelves north and south, shelves east and west—you name it, they tried it. Big signs, small unique wrought-iron signs, lighted signs, reflective signs. None of it worked. Some were under-funded, some inept, some lacked knowledge in the retail business, but none had a proven system or method of running a store of this kind.

How Systems Can Help You Get There From Here

In your work or in the organization you belong to, you may be resisting the restrictions and the rules that you have to live with. If you belong to a franchise, you have a greater chance of survival (success) than if you strike out on your own. A franchise is a system.

Most people have jobs or are part of some form of organizational structure. Most people balk at the strictures and mores that they think keep them from reaching what they think is their full potential, or at least from getting the creative latitude they feel they need in order to do what they would like to do.

Don't Waste Your Time Re-Inventing the Wheel

One really needs to think twice about starting anything from scratch today. There is plenty of room to be creative, but before you spend tons of money and put in endless nights in front of your computer, check to see if it's already been done. Perhaps you can join a group or company that has large resources that allow you to independently do your thing within its framework or system. I am ferociously independent and freedom oriented, but I have learned how much more freedom you can have if you plug into a well-oiled existing entity that provides much of what you need in order to help make your business or organization work. That may be software, product fulfillment, literature, audio visuals, etc. and many are already done or at least customizable for your use.

Once you understand the value of a good system and learn how to put your ego aside to work with it, the rewards can be astounding. It can even give you the very thing you want most—freedom!

Once you understand the value of a good system and learn how to put your ego aside to work with it, the rewards can be astounding. It can even give you the very thing you want most—freedom!

What Is a System?

Systems are a way of doing business or running an organization.

You are most likely part of someone else's system, or you are trying to run one. Both are fraught with great difficulty and hours of angst. But when the understanding of the system prevails, the clouds lift, the skies clear, and you are at peace with yourself and those around you.

If you are an intense and persistent back-seat driver, you are in for rough time. Some people find it impossible to follow something that someone else developed or created. If they didn't come up with it, they don't know how to play. If you are someone who has to do it your way, or thinks you have to fix everyone or everything, and you are in a system or even just in a relationship, you are most likely not having a good time right now. In fact, you may not have ulcers, but you for sure are a carrier. So why use a system?

Three-Part Summary of Systems

This is not theory for me. I have run large systems with thousands of people under my tutelage. I have also been, and I am currently, part of a large and dynamic system with even more individuals involved.

1. Why a System?

Let's consider again that competing store up the road from us that changed hands every 18 months or so. Each owner went broke trying to rectify what they thought were the previous owner's mistakes. In comparison, up the road in the other direction was the 7/11, which started about the same time. It flourished for the whole 30 years that we lived in the area.

Even the most relaxed-looking organizations like Microsoft have a system. There's no possible way to succeed with longevity or to affectively duplicate concepts within a large organization without one. Basically it's your code of conduct, your method of doing things, your way of relating to each other, and the way you present yourself to the world. It becomes your stock-in-trade—your very heartbeat. It's the thing that creates clarity, efficiency, productivity, profitability and peace of mind for those who buy in. They know what they are all about.

Every successful sports team has a system. Every good coach has a system, as does every good franchise.

Recently I heard of two young guns who arrived at an NHL (National Hockey League) training camp and immediately began challenging the coach on his system. Not good at your first team meeting. They never even saw the ice. They were gone packing the first day. That may be a bit severe, but the moral is clear: earn a few stripes first.

The more clarification a system has, the more those involved are willing to commit to it, and the smoother the organization runs. It takes a strong leader at the helm to make it work, a leader who is inclusive in the process of making major decisions, and rewards people for "getting" it. That system makes it through even the worst storm.

The more clarification a system has, the more those involved are willing to commit to it, and the smoother the organization runs.

Team members who take ownership of the system are given a lot more ice time, stage time or recognition and responsibilities in their chosen field than those who don't. They also have a lot more independence and a lot more say in decision-making. If this upsets you, you have a problem. You're probably not a team player, which means you may never become one. You may just be on your own, and that's okay; you can still make it. Good luck.

Team members who take ownership of the system are given a lot more ice time, stage time or recognition and responsibilities in their chosen field than those who don't.

Even as a leader of a system, you have to be a good team player because the cards don't always fall your way. The need to be inclusive of your key players while making big decisions is vital if you want to safely and effectively captain the ship across deep and often troubled waters. A captain of a big ship has many people he or she must trust, depend on and give authority to. You constantly have to deal with the fine balance between empowerment and abdication. You also constantly deal with this balance while you are systematically leading, managing, and strategizing your way to the ultimate prize. You don't need these skills for a skiff or a row boat, but you do need them for a big ship.

2. How to Run a System

Obviously, in the short "Cliffs Notes" version of these subjects, we're not going to give a full exposé of how to run a system. Neither do I presume that I have all the answers to this question. At another time and place I would like to do a complete and in-depth treatise of this subject with friends of mine who have more experience than I do with the subject. But this will give you a good idea of what's involved.

We start with ourselves. If we don't have a system for running our personal lives in the areas of personal hygiene, dress, a time to go to bed and a time to get up, and keeping our surroundings consistently neat and tidy, our car reasonably clean, our attitude positive, and our chequebook balanced, we will have difficulty running the world. I think we may have several world leaders trying to manage these activities now!

The best way to learn how to run a system is to be part of one, and when you became a good team player you can think about loftier things if you still aspire to that goal. The best leaders are the best followers. There have been thousands of books written about leadership, many by people who only have a theoretical experience of the subject, or who confuse management with leadership. That's a different subject.

> "The best way to learn how to run a system is to be part of one, and when you became a good team player you can think about loftier things if you still aspire to that goal.

If you are leading or aspire to, or if you have oversight of a group of people or of entities involving people, you most likely already are engaged in some form of system. It begins with a framework that defines who you are, what you do, and how you want the world to see you.

After that, a system is defined by "how we do things here," usually through manuals, training sessions, CDs, DVDs, MP3 downloads, and social media of all kinds. On-the-job training brings focus to the system or the method of doing business.

Running a system begins with having one to run. In other words, having a following and then a "clearly defined method" of doing everything that you do in your organization:

1. The vital signs or the activity levels that are expected or necessary to achieve various levels of productivity.
2. Providing outlines, PowerPoints or DVDs for routine presentations.
3. Providing the tools to do the job, i.e., literature, brochures, manuals, CDs, MP3 downloads, websites and instructions on how to use every kind of communication tool available, including social networking tools such as YouTube, Facebook, Twitter etc.
4. Instructions and guidelines on the proper use of smart phones, e.g., Blackberries, iPhones, etc.
5. Types of meetings and presentations, and who presides over them: how to expense them and how to recover the cost. A system won't thrive or survive long term without seminars, conferences, awards, recognition and incentives.
6. Nurturing people and making them feel like they belong is the number-one desire of people in an organization. Provide it, in this order: belonging, recognition, security, freedom, money and working conditions.
7. Travel instructions, from how to book travel to save thousands of dollars a year, to behaviour, ethics and even moral standards on the road.
8. The attitudes and principles of the organization, e.g., edification is a key factor here. Do we build people up or tear them down? Do we always look at things with the glass half full or half empty? This is an old,

overused, trite statement, but it's a huge factor in how well a group moves forward.

9. The effective and disciplined use of social media of all kinds is a key factor today in being a relevant system.

The engine of every organization begins and ends with its core competency. You should be able to explain what you do in one sentence. It's called the elevator speech. It helps you measure your progress. At the end of the day, did we move forward in the direction of the goals and purposes of our business or organization?

3. How to Operate within a System

This is very difficult for some people. Stubborn, self-willed, self-centred, rebellious, narcissistic people don't do well being part of someone else's "way of doing things." This does not mean they are not able to succeed; they're just not likely to succeed within a system.

There must be a measure of humility and submission to do well here. If one can imagine working within a known successful business or organizational system, the rewards can be amazing. As previously mentioned, a well-run system provides a place to belong as well.

1. Lifelong relationships and friendships of unparalleled proportion are forged.
2. A system allows one to be recognized, at times in front of many people in huge and spectacular venues. You cannot do that by yourself.
3. There is security in numbers and in belonging to a group of like-minded people.
4. Without a system one must always be responsible and fully engaged. In a system there are many team leaders to help carry the load, giving much freedom

to each member. The system becomes the source, rather than any one individual. Everyone plugs into the source, lightening the load for everyone. Let me not mislead you into thinking that it is possible to be passive and still succeed, or that individual effort is not needed. Never.

5. Working conditions are always better within a well-oiled system.

The biggest issue is learning to be a team player. Putting *the* business or *the* team ahead of your business translates as adjusting one's own schedule to the schedule of the system and using the system's tools and functions.

On the surface, this seems very restrictive and dictatorial, but in fact it is actually very freeing. It allows you to participate but not be exclusively responsible for creating or initiating all of the training, the tools and the functions. Instead, you can utilize these to leverage and therefore magnify and multiply every effort you put into building your business and your future. As a trusted team player you will also have lots of input to the process.

So now you have had a look at systems from 35,000 feet. This just barely gives a cursory view of what we are prescribing here. So be diligent in your pursuit of an entity with a great system behind it, one that has stood the test of time and has many fulfilled and successful leaders and many followers in it.

So be diligent in your pursuit of an entity with a great system behind it, one that has stood the test of time and has many fulfilled and successful leaders and many followers in it.

A
Rendezvous
with
Destiny

The King's Speech

Included in King George VI's famous Christmas speech in 1939 was this epigraph sent to him by a Canadian lady by the name of Minnie Louise Haskins.

It read:

I said to the man who stood at the gate of the year, "Give me a light that I may tread safely into the unknown." He replied, "Go into the darkness and put your hand into the hand of God. That shall be to you better than a light and safer than a known way."

Chapter 23: When Destiny Calls

Almost everyone has within them a calling, a purpose and a reason for passing this way.

Finding the path to your destiny starts with some very basic things. The path is not as profound, ethereal or difficult to discover as we often make it. Just because destiny calls, however, does not necessarily mean it will be fulfilled either. We have to hear the call and answer it.

In these tumultuous times, life still goes on and many people accomplish great things, even though they may have troubling and traumatic experiences in their personal and corporate lives along the way.

I'm Going Away to Find Myself

I've seldom heard great revelations come from individuals who went away to "find" themselves. If we haven't had that rendezvous with destiny, hopefully a time comes in our lives that we find meaningful and fulfilling. When this time arrives, it usually is not about us, but the result of how we are significantly affecting the lives of those around us. That is our destiny and our legacy.

Many people can't find their calling because they are desperately looking for personal fulfillment and gratification, or are just striving to survive. Destiny doesn't live there. So often, folks are looking for fulfillment in all the wrong places.

> Many people can't find their calling because they are desperately looking for personal fulfillment and gratification, or are just striving to survive. Destiny doesn't live there.

What helped me was discovering a core set of beliefs that gave me a centredness that was worth sharing with others and could bring others to a better place in their lives. My goal for the past 45 years has been to help people become more than they are, to help them find that joy-filled inner peace that passes all understanding, to find a focus for their lives that may or may not be part of their vocation. People who have these interwoven into their lives are fortunate, but that doesn't happen all that often.

Seven Areas of Fulfillment

It really helps if you can find a vehicle, as in a career path, which includes fulfillment in all areas of your life. If you are fortunate enough, you find an opportunity that provides:

1. A sense of belonging
2. An appreciation and recognition for outstanding achievement
3. A measure of security (to know that the money part of your life is taken care of)
4. Freedom (to spend several months a year on vacation with family and friends, or travel, and so on.)
5. Adequate cash flow
6. Your desired lifestyle
7. Significance

Ideally, people want these seven things from their vocation. This scenario is not that easy to find. Many of those seeking these types of opportunities encounter a lot of unfulfilled promises and broken dreams along the way. The vehicle oftentimes is not a mainstream vehicle, and it requires the willingness to be different. You need to do what your peers, your friends and acquaintances may not be willing to do. You may walk alone for a short time until you find those who have found the same path.

Wealth and Fame

So often we equate success or our ultimate fulfillment with wealth or fame. I know many people who enjoy all seven things, and also many who do not and never will benefit from these in their lifetime. My father is one of them. He was a schoolteacher and administrator all of his working life. At 95 years of age, he still enjoyed a most amazingly fulfilled and satisfying life, in which all the fulfillment areas mentioned have been resident and fully alive in his life. He found his destiny in education and pursued it diligently and successfully for 40-plus years. Unfortunately he just passed away last week and we will miss him very much. He was a great example of all that we have discussed here.

Once you can picture what fulfillment looks like for you, do not wait for it to come to you—go for it with great gusto, even if it turns into great wealth or fame. Rather than turn wealth and fame down, use it for the good of your fellow man, as did David, Solomon, Joseph, Job, Abraham and Jacob. Humble, generous, wealthy and famous people do an enormous amount of good as they pass this way.

> Rather than turn wealth and fame down, use it for the good of your fellow man. Humble, generous, wealthy and famous people do an enormous amount of good as they pass this way.

When you find your core focus and belief system, you may find yourself one day, as I did a few months ago, in the middle of a busy lobby of a prestigious hotel. I was there with a couple of East Indian friends, who asked me to pray with them because of the devastating sudden death of their dear friend and business associate that morning. Our backgrounds and religious beliefs are vastly different, so why would they ask me to do that? Their core beliefs are solid and they know that my core beliefs are solid. So we could be enjoined in a moment of grief, uninhibited by our differences, to ask our Creator to give comfort and peace in a very distraught time in their lives. Obviously, there was also a great deal of trust present. We talk about trust in a later chapter.

These two buddies and I have a genuine friendship and respect for each other because we've worked side by side for several years on a board of directors during some very stressful times. All of this precedes and supersedes any differences, as was demonstrated by our shared tears in that special huddle that has bonded us as even greater friends. They also saw that time of bonding as a special moment in our lives.

It may seem strange to some of you, but when one knows who they are and knows what their destiny looks like, amazing things can happen without any compromise or loss of focus. You might see things like this happening to other people and think those kinds of things will never happen to you. That is probably true, but you will enjoy other amazing life experiences that are unique to your life exclusively.

> " It may seem strange to some of you, but when one knows who they are and knows what their destiny looks like, amazing things can happen without any compromise or loss of focus.

It Takes 10,000 Hours

In most cases, to successfully become a fulfilled person in a given area or discipline, you need to invest up to 10,000 hours, or about five years, honing your trade, profession, or gifting. Even then, if you just stay there, you fade away.

I like flying with a pilot who has flown 10,000 hours. If I was slated for an operation, I would like to be operated on by a surgeon with 10,000 hours, or at least five years of experience. But I am also thankful for the younger set that are there, gaining their experience and using their youthful skills, while standing on the shoulders of those who have gone before.

The goal for the rest of our lives must be to influence others with what we have learned and are continuing to learn, so we can affect those around us with our knowledge, our skills, our crafts, and our caring for a lifetime.

The goal for the rest of our lives must be to influence others with what we have learned and are continuing to learn, so we can affect those around us with our knowledge, our skills, our crafts, and our caring for a lifetime.

I hear too many songs these days dominated by personal pronouns. They're missing it! It may be better to sing someone else's song and learn from their lyrics until you have your own meaningful song to sing. I call these songs 7/11 songs: 7 words sung 11 times.

A person wrapped up in themselves makes a very small package and a very small life to go with it. Centering ourselves around others, and allowing ourselves to be mentored by experience and greatness, is the key to maturity and to reaching one's destiny with fewer disruptions. It may seem too slow for some, but in the end it is much more expeditious.

A person wrapped up in themself makes a very small package and a very small life to go with it.

Boating has been a passion of mine for my entire life, and the secret to success in ocean boating is mentorship. A friend came out from Manitoba to the West Coast, and with no ocean boating experience, he set off across the bay with his family for a gorgeous day on the water. Within minutes, the boat was grounded on a sand bar and he and the family had to stay there for hours until the tide came up to free them. Hungry, sunburned and fatigued, he learned his lesson.

Ego has been described by some as Edging God Out. Ego and greed are the biggest reasons for the demise of those who've risen to great heights. Ego and Greed can drive a person to temporary success and momentary fame and fulfillment, but that most often comes to an abrupt end.

> Ego has been described by some as Edging God Out. Ego and greed are the biggest reasons for the demise of those who've risen to great heights.

Jim Collins, who wrote *Good to Great*, a book I hold in high regard, also wrote *How the Mighty Fall*. There is a proverb that says, "Therefore let anyone who thinks that he stands take heed lest he fall." Just look at yesteryear's mighty—where are most of them today? There is a natural ebb and flow of life that we must accept.

At 70 I understand this, but there are still too many unnecessary, premature, and painful crashes that could be avoided if certain warning signs were observed.

In his second book, *How the Mighty Fall*, Jim Collins says, "Every institution, no matter how great, is vulnerable to decline." No law of nature exists promising that the most powerful will remain at the top. Anyone can fall and many eventually do, but as Collins emphasises, "Some companies do indeed recover and in some cases, come back stronger, even after having crashed into the depths...."

Watch for Pot Holes While Looking to Fulfill Your Destiny

The five stages of decline according to Collins are:

Stage 1: Hubris Born of Success (Hubris being arrogance and pride)
Stage 2: Undisciplined Pursuit of More
Stage 3: Denial of Risk and Peril
Stage 4: Grasping for Salvation (Survival)
Stage 5: Capitulation to Irrelevance...

I recommend reading this book for advice which could be invaluable to you.

Failure can be avoided or staved off if warning signs are heeded. Ultimate destiny can only be achieved by those who finish well. It seems like a long and tedious road, but I've worked with those who stayed true to the end and with those who were deterred by distractions along the way. Life was 100 percent better for those who lived their lives intentionally right to their last days.

These are the people who stayed in the game without losing focus of the destiny they were called to. Even though this destiny was not always directly tied to their vocation, it was and is in most cases at least complemented by it.

> Failure can be avoided or staved off if warning signs are heeded. Ultimate destiny can only be achieved by those who finish well.

Most who attempted to conquer the world were eventually crushed by it, and often by the same devices they used to attempt to conquer it.

"What shall it profit a man if he shall gain the whole world, and lose his own soul?"

You might say, "I don't get it—this sounds like a fearful and de-motivating message. What is the point of trying to achieving anything if it inevitably ends in failure?"

Okay, ingest the following, I unapologetically say,

1. Be as healthy as you can
2. Make as much money as you can
3. Give as much as you can
4. Save as much as you can
5. While simultaneously making a difference in as many lives as you can
6. Obey the rules—get into the winners' circle and stay in there as long as you can
7. You will be a person of influence

I believe everyone is born with the seeds of "greatness." Greatness is achieved by someone who brings meaning and fulfillment to themselves and others. A person could achieve greatness while living on the filthy streets of Calcutta as Mother Teresa did, or by touching the lives of people right in your neighbourhood who need a hand up.

Go flat out with whatever you have been given to do, and if you are joyous while doing it, you find your destiny in there somewhere. Staring at the stars seldom achieves anything unless you are an astronomer. "Whatever your hand finds to do, do it with all your might!" Do it with solid moral principles and continue to live by them; and you will be "like a tree planted by the streams of living water, and everything you do will prosper." Need more? Read Psalms, Chapter One.

> Staring at the stars seldom achieves anything unless you are an astronomer.

Don't Wait

So go flat out with what's in your hands without waiting until the total clarity of your purpose and destiny has been revealed, because it may never come to you the way you expect it. I know many people who felt like their purpose in life never came into focus, but who lived very successful and fulfilling lives. I've also seen people who've only realized what a difference they made after years of being diligent with what they had in their hands. That was their destiny!

It Is a Decision I Made This Morning

Many people ask me why I have such a consistently upbeat disposition. I say, "It is a decision I made this morning." I think most of us are called to do the above. The happiest people I know are the ones who are "giving it" every day. The complainers and the "down chunkers" are a drag on society. We have a choice to be part of the problem or part of the solution every day, because most of what life hands us comes from the decisions we make.

There are three levels of maturity. They are:

1. Please help me—Some people like to skip this one, but don't.
2. I can handle it—You can, with your mentor's help.
3. Please let me help you—Becomes the theme for the rest of your life when maturity kicks in, if leadership or influence of any kind is your calling.

We must work through all three, if we are to move confidently and knowledgably to the fulfillment of our respective purpose, goals and dreams—our destiny.

"The greatest day in your life and mine is when we take total responsibility for our attitudes. That's the day we truly grow up."
John Maxwell

Intention about All Areas of Life

To live with our destiny in mind, we need to be intentional about all areas of our lives. They are all keys to fulfilling it. Once we have settled on who we are and why we are here, we can commit to a new reality of extending our boundaries, discovering meaningful experiences, and then just flat out taking care of business, and working hard at our present vocation, and in all other areas of our lives.

Vocation

We often talk about our chosen vocation or profession, yet many of us never chose it. It was just a job that put groceries on the table and you never left it. Or maybe you didn't know which avenue to pursue and you've just gone from job to job and hoped for the best. I find university grads almost as unfocused as those who never graduated or never did post-secondary education.

You can live life on purpose or by accident—you decide. I wanted summers off by the water, so I became a teacher with summers off, in addition to Easter or spring break and Christmas break. Freedom was my major mantra, so when I went into business, I made sure it would grow to be a semi-absentee independent ownership deal. This way, I could have, guess what—summers by the water and much of the winter in the sun as well. I also could always be with family and friends and business associates, as I thrive on having people around. It's been an amazing life and just gets better.

Finances

Please refer to chapter 5.

Physical

We all know we have a lot to do to keep up a physical fitness routine on purpose. I've not always won at this and now am working to recover "the years the locusts have eaten." Eating properly and exercising every day is a short statement but a life-long vigil. So many folks find themselves in a physical funk that they have trouble getting out of.

There is a huge amount of good information on wellness out there today. Here's a real mini nutshell. It's a quick and dirty formula for healthy eating:

- Nothing white (no refined sugar, no white bread, even whole wheat, and very light on dairy).
- Stay away from packaged foods as much as possible.
- Lots of fruits and vegetables
- Easy on the orange juice
- No pop
- Easy on the coffee

A simple day may look like this:

1. Have a good breakfast. Include protein (eggs) and a small bowl of berries
2. Snack if you need one (carrots and celery are the best). A 160-or-less-calorie protein food bar will do if you are on the run
3. Lunch—a good-sized salad with chicken or tuna if you wish, and an apple
4. Snack as above
5. Dinner—salmon, lean beef or turkey patties, salad and fruit

6. Light snack no later than 8:00 PM

Social

Have a network of friends that you do things with. Go to shows, play cards, spend a day at the beach, go out to dinner, plan special dinners at home. You name it. These activities are all very important for your well-being.

Spiritual

We have discussed this before and I won't belabour the point, but you have a soul. Feed it.

Family

We all know the value of a good family. Be the one who makes it better.

Recreation

This is vital for a well-rounded life. Find something that's not work-related and have fun doing it.

Significance

We have done this one already. Make your life others-centred. Do something every day for others, even if it just the gift of a smile or a pleasant greeting. We soon begin to realize the benefits, rewards and blessings that can be ours.

You have a soul. Feed it.

Chapter 24: Perspective Is Needed if Destiny is to Be Achieved

The amount of ignorance that abounds these days is appalling. If we only allow ourselves to live on our street and never venture out into the bigger world, our perspective doesn't allow us to understand where others come from. The poor and those who feel victimized have just as much responsibility to understand those whom they see as their oppressors as those who supposedly are their oppressors. The latter must get out of their ivory towers and see what it's really like on the streets below.

I have friends and relatives who have deliberately lived for a week or a weekend amongst the lowest of society, sleeping in homeless shelters and getting food where the street people get theirs. This is life-changing for them and allows compassion to take on new meaning.

Having and Getting Perspective

A wonderful surgeon friend of mine often says when someone gets really off track or speaks out of turn, "Would you just hold your water!" Being a bit of a redneck, he also says in a totally different context, "We get asked out often but usually only once."

We could fill a bunch of pages with stories and illustrations of perspective. Recently I have been reading books written by people whom I know have a different perspective from mine, just to round out my education and at times be introduced to a larger, more inclusive view of issues that I have been pretty set on for years.

If I only communicate from my narrow viewpoint or understanding of how the world turns, no matter what that may be, I won't be as credible as I should be or want to be. So I'm not yet ready to launch out into a full on discussion of perspectives, other than to say we may want to ask questions and try to see things through as many lenses as possible before we express our views on issues that we may not be that familiar with.

Finances

Too many people today don't realize they are responsible for this piece of life's puzzle.

Basically you have to make a living, so as part of your passion or dream, you must determine the lifestyle you wish to have, and then find ways to make that happen financially. Too many miss this part of the equation and then everything comes apart at the seams, or worse yet, never comes together in the first place. You always need to be making a living at something until your dream or opportunity comes together for you. If your ship isn't coming in, start swimming out towards it.

> You always need to be making a living at something until your dream or opportunity comes together for you. If your ship isn't coming in, start swimming out towards it.

I have never missed a day of work in my life. Why? At first I couldn't afford to be without work, and later I loved every moment of my involvement in my various enterprises over the past 50 years—I still do. I started working in a bookstore in my grade 6 year. I had a substantial paper route after that. Then I worked on a crew building sidewalks, worked on farms, on the railroad, built fences, worked in a service station, a sawmill as a tail sawyer and on road construction driving huge earthmovers at the age of 18 and 19 on 12 hour shifts from 7 p.m. to 7 a.m. all summer. Then at 20, I was in the classroom teaching school, and by 22 I became a small businessman and later ended up helping many non-profit organizations raise millions along their way.

Balance

To have a life full of all that it can offer, a balance must exist and all the elements of life and living need be in play. Are you the CEO of all the departments of your life? Is it balanced and fulfilled, incorporating all elements? No one has this down perfectly for sure. We just keep trying to get as close to that perfection line as possible.

Our Physical Well-being

Unless we work at this intentionally, health and wellness is thwarted. I had years of vibrant health, and then some years when I failed miserably at being intentional about my health and fitness. I paid the price. Now I'm back at it. Our bodies are fearfully and wonderfully made by design, and so by a designer. Some lower level of intelligence keeps groping for an unanswered story to our creation, our existence and our future. I encourage it because the more they study with open minds, the more they come to the truth without any brainwashing or arm twisting. Great scientists are acknowledging truth on a regular basis now, as they open their minds to what the universe clearly spells out to them.

The universe declares the glory of God. This all has to do with knowing that you know, not blindly, but eventually with new eyes.

The universe declares the glory of God. This all has to do with knowing that you know, not blindly but eventually with new eyes.

Our Profession or Chosen Occupation

Finding something that is going to pay the bills and have as many of the elements I talked about earlier is the goal. We should not settle for second best if possible. We should keep a roof over our heads while we keep searching for what will give us satisfaction in our profession or career. It's out there, but these days it pays to proceed with caution, because many "opportunities" are only beneficial to those offering them. If you have to pay any substantial amount up front, really put on the brakes! There are so many ways to research thoroughly these days via the Internet. You probably have a theme for your life. You probably already have your 10,000 hours in, you just have to find a way to package and market your worth to the market place. You may have to start at the bottom of something you really want to do and work hard to move up to the spot that intrigues you.

These poignant elements make up our entire lives.

There are many more inspiring stories. I leave you with one of my favourites, as told by an NHL hockey player, Ryan Walter:

How Great Ones Drive Success

"According to *Sports Leaders & Success: 55 Top Sports Leaders & How They Achieved Greatness,* a panel of 50 hockey experts ranked Wayne Gretzky as the top player in the history of the game of hockey. Gretzky held or shared 61 National

Hockey League offensive records by the time he retired in 1999, including most career goals (894), most assists (1,963) and most total points (2,857). He was justifiably inducted into the Hockey Hall of Fame just seven months after he retired.

"Gretzky's potential was obvious at a very young age, but Wayne shares in his autobiography that his parents kept him grounded with phrases like: 'Don't get bigheaded on me,' or, 'No matter how good you are, there's always someone better.' Gretzky's father taught Wayne that he needed to be held to a higher standard than other players because of his giftedness, and he needed to always put forth an effort that matched his ability.

"Wayne failed to put that effort into practice the day after the Oilers lost the third game of the 1983 Stanley Cup finals to the New York Islanders. Wayne's father reminded him of this later that summer during a family visit to Gretzky's grandmother, while watching her working in her garden: 'Look at that. She's 79, and she's still working hard,' his father pointed out. 'You're 23, and when you're in the Stanley Cup finals, you won't even practice! People are going to judge you on how you perform every night. Never forget that.'

"I am not sure how many of you know this, but I played with Wayne Gretzky on Canada's National Junior Team in 1978. Were any of you born yet? I captained that team. We were surprised during training camp by a young 16-year-old from Ontario who not only made our team when most of us were 19 years old, but then went on to lead the World Junior Tournament in scoring.

"During each of my 15 NHL seasons I played against Wayne Gretzky. He was not always the most talented player on the ice, but he was the most consistently competitive player every time. Wayne was hungry!"

Conclusion

Well, there you have it.

In these chapters you've been given mostly an accumulation of thoughts and ideas that have helped us along the way to any successes we have had. It's been a very rewarding journey that certainly had many exclamation points as we rendezvoused with destiny several times over these few short 70-plus years.

Don't worry about your destiny. It is unfolding as it should as long as you prudently move forward with the hand you've been dealt every day. Expect great things to happen and they will. Know that things you never dreamed of are waiting for you up ahead, regardless of today's circumstances. Live fully in the precious present and revel in the great future that you have yet to experience.

> Expect great things to happen and they will. Know that things you never dreamed of are waiting for you up ahead, regardless of today's circumstances. Live fully in the precious present and revel in the great future that you have yet to experience.

Squandering opportunities is more common than not having them in the first place, but if you've done that, don't live there, just move on. Thoughts are so powerful and determine so much of what our lives look like today and, more importantly, what they will look like tomorrow. Intentional living is so crucial to our future. What we seriously intend to do is so vital to the most minute details of our lives.

Never give up on the belief that you have a destiny to fulfill. Dare to find it, dare to discover it, dare to fulfill it.

Dare to find it, dare to discover it, dare to fulfill it.

Final Thoughts

I left as much on the cutting floor as I put into these pages. Much of it didn't quite fit this theme but is still vital to life and living. So we might go again sometime with crazy, exciting, and sometimes hair-raising stories and intense and miraculous circumstances, and with some of the amazing outcomes that have dotted these seven decades.

I two-finger-typed this whole manuscript on planes, in hotel rooms and mostly in my spacious den, where the thoughts seem to flow best. Next time I record and someone else types.

I hope that, as we have poked and prodded our way through this, something meaningful has been said to help you focus more diligently on your purpose, dream or desire. On your way to your rendezvous with destiny, may you find greater significance as you make a difference in the lives of others.

Blessing—James E. Janz

References

Askew, Gloria. *The Secret of Supplements*

The Bible

Bristol, Claude M. *The Magic of Believing*

Collins, Jim. *Good to Great*

Collins, Jim. *How the Mighty Fall*

Conwell, Russell H. *Acres of Diamonds*

Hill, Napoleon. *Think and Grow Rich*

Kiyosaki, Robert. *Rich Dad Poor Dad*

Maltz, Maxwell. *Psycho-Cybernetics*

Nightingale, Earl. *The Strangest Secret* (LP)

Peale, Norman Vincent. *The Power of Positive Thinking*

Robertson, Pat. *The Secret Kingdom*

Schuller, Robert H. *Move Ahead with Possibility Thinking*

Schwartz, David. *The Magic of Thinking Big*

Stone, William Clement. *The Success System that Never Fails*

Walter, Ryan. *Hungry!*

Wilkinson, Bruce. *The Dream Giver*

A Rendezvous with Destiny